DARK PSYCHOLOGY AND MANIPULATION

Master The Art Of Persuasion, Use Nlp And Body Language To Influence People, And See Through The Mind Control Tricks Of Narcissists And Manipulators

Conrad Harmon

processes, or directions contained within is the solitary and utter responsibility of the recipient reader. Under no circumstances will any legal responsibility or blame be held against the publisher for any reparation, damages, or monetary loss due to the information herein, either directly or indirectly.

Respective authors own all copyrights not held by the publisher.

The information herein is offered for informational purposes solely, and is universal as so. The presentation of the information is without contract or any type of guarantee assurance.

The trademarks that are used are without any consent, and the publication of the trademark is without permission or backing by the trademark owner. All trademarks and brands within this book are for clarifying purposes only and are the owned by the owners themselves, not affiliated with this document

TABLE OF CONTENTS

CHAPTER 1
INTRODUCTION TO THE ART OF DARK PSYCHOLOGY

What is Dark Psychology?

They say that know-how is electricity. Nicely, if knowledge is strength, then knowing human psychology is the equal to that of getting notable powers. Psychology, the understanding of the human mind and the way it works, is a topic relevant to the existence of humanity. It underpins the whole lot from advertising to finance, crime to religion, and love to hate. A person who understands mental standards holds the key to human effect on a vital few different humans.

Obtaining mental expertise is just a hard project like several of humanity's most advanced secrets and techniques. Psychological understanding is buried deep within the pages of dense journals and stored out of the reach of the general public. To distill these adequate records into a useful shape might require a person to delve through countless books and journals; trying to separate the valuable from the vain.

That procedure has been completed! You are studying a contemporary distillation of several the most potent principles inside the global of psychology. You don't need any unique knowledge to take something away from this eBook, only a willingness to learn, replicate, and apply your new expertise.

The book you currently possess gives perception into a hidden global understanding that few humans realize and even fewer recognize even with knowledge. The sector of "Dark Psychology," those are the principles and procedures used by the greatest powerful influencers the arena has ever acknowledged. You have got a ticket to discover many of human history's most devious minds and the diabolical ideas they devised.

No longer will you be presented insight into the standards undermining what amounts to black mental magic, you will be proven the methods claimed in the principles which can be carried out by any individual.

In addition, that's not all. Actual lifestyle case studies are provided as examples, so you can apprehend those thoughts with the aid of seeing how surely, they were used for the duration of history.

Why do you want to Understand Dark Psychology?

Dark psychology is at paintings within the world. You may not like this truth, but you can't deny it. That you have a choice: either try to remain ignorant to something so powerful and risk it turning you into its next victim or take control of your situation. Learn how to protect yourself and those you love, from folks that would smash you via their ruthless psychological tricks.

Expertise in Dark psychology isn't always the most effective defensive measure. There are ideas and principles contained within the world of Dark psychology that assist you in getting ahead on your private and professional endeavors. No one is looking for you to end up a psychopath; however, without a doubt, you may use a little extra energy in your everyday existence.

With Extraordinary Electricity Comes First-rate Responsibility

How you use this information is up to you. It could be the most effective psychological knowledge you have ever encountered. Becoming a weapon used to give you an advantage in life. The ideas and examples contained in this book are tools. Use them to build whatever kind of life you desire.

This eBook isn't for the faint of heart or the weak minded As soon as you have lifted the curtain on the world of Dark psychology, there may be no going back. You may have the know-how of human nature that few have ever received. With superb energy comes superb responsibility. You have been warned.

What's Covert Emotional Manipulation?

It is no twist of fate that covert emotional manipulation, also known as CEM, is featured first on this eBook. Most of the Dark psychology strategies you will encounter employ this kind of emotional manipulation in one form or another. As you examine the world of Dark psychology and its various manifestations, you will understand the symptoms of CEM. Knowledge precisely of what CEM includes is consequently, a vital first step in understanding Dark psychology.

Covert emotional manipulation is the attempt by one individual to steer the thoughts and emotions of every other in an underhand manner; this is subtle by the individual being manipulated. Breaking down each of the three phrases inside the identity is an excellent manner to get to cope with this foundational concept.

Covert refers to the manner some manipulators can hide their intentions and the actual nature of their actions. Not all emotional manipulation and affect can be categorized as covert. Victims of the covert type but will typically not understand they have been manipulated. Not be able to recognize the manner of manipulation that has been executed and will no longer be able to guess on the motivation in their manipulator. CEM is a mental stealth bomber, fending off detection and defense until it's too late.

The emotional aspect of the manipulation refers to the specific attention of the manipulator. Different forms of viable manipulation consist of human beings behaviors, ideals, and strength of will.

CEM focuses on impacting a person's emotional country and fact. Many manipulators' attention in this vicinity of affecting as they know someone's feelings are the key to all different aspects of their character. Manipulating someone's feelings is like cutting off a person's oxygen supply without them noticing, until it is too late. If someone has learnt emotional management, they have got full control.

The last piece of this puzzle is the term "Manipulation." It is a commonplace false impression that has an impact on, and manipulation are the same component; that is not the case. Manipulation refers to the sneaky and hidden actions of affecting that takes area outside the awareness of the individual can manage. The aim of influencing someone as opposed to the intention at the end of manipulating them is another critical difference.

An influencer has the mind-set of "I would like to help you make decisions which can be desirable for you." A manipulator has the mentality of "I need to manipulate you to give an advantage to myself secretly." Consequently, information the goal in the back of any given behavior is in abundant element identifying whether it's miles an example of covert emotional manipulation or no longer.

Now, you have got an overview of precisely what covert emotional manipulation is and how it differs from other styles of influence and management. The most likely to occur situations tin order to locate covert emotional manipulation taking place will now be explored, as well as the primary types of manipulative characters that arise time and time again.

Conditions and Manipulators

Plainly speaking, there are four primary situations where covert emotional manipulation can take effect. Those are the expert, non-public, romantic, and family circles of life. Poetic covert emotional manipulation is perhaps the most common situation and can be the most lethal. Less apparent kinds of CEM may be discovered nearly everywhere. After you apprehend the idea and the sensible programs of it, you will be able to guard towards it, regardless of what scenario you find yourself in.

Just as there are everyday situations where covert emotional manipulation can arise, there are not unusual forms of folks that take place the ideas undermining

CEM. Being capable of implementing the idea of CEM to actual, non-public portrayals of its purposes is a critical aspect of understanding it.

A controlling romantic companion is a standard private portrayal of the principles of CEM. If a person is courting and their companion is trying to control them, the individual is likely to be disgusted by what is going on and seeking to discover a manner out of the situation. For that reason, many controlling partners exercise their effect in the sneakiest way possible. Their girlfriend or spouse finally ends up being a victim of total emotional manipulation without ever figuring out it's far taking place. This offers the manipulator; what they desire without any of the dangers of being discovered and losing the other person for the top.

A so-called "Buddy" may additionally make use of CEM to get the end results, them out of their relationship with every other person. In this case, one of the most extreme, common behavior of the manipulator is a person who covertly introduces a close friend the feelings of guilt, sympathy, and obligation in the direction of them. The buddy who's being manipulated in this way may be unaware that they're being manipulated They will not be able to explain why they act and behave the way they do around them, "Buddy," the manipulator.

The expert domain is any other common playground for covert emotional manipulators. Countless human beings have memories of getting labored for an MD, or different person of authority, which resulted in triggering mysterious feelings of guilt, worry, or duty in them. People who've been manipulated in this manner should in no way pick out why those emotions exist or where they come from.

Individual family examples are some of the most complex examples inside the global of CEM. A professional manipulator who can pick out a victim within their circle of relatives is very dangerous in ways of manipulation they can manage. This is due to the truth that CEM is an effective approach even when the manipulator and sufferer have an undeniable connection to each other. While the genuine connection of blood relation is introduced into the mix, the level of manage and influence can increase exponentially.

Why are family conditions so applicable to using

CEM? Virtually positioned, humans already feel a level of social duty to help human beings out of their family and "Move the more mile" to make certain their wishes are attended to. This current predisposition toward influence is brought to with the aid of the covert emotional manipulative practices and the end results are a malleable victim.

How exactly do covert emotional manipulators manage to instill such degrees of manipulating over their victims? They have more than a few tactics that are difficult to detect or even harder to resist without the knowledge to protect yourself. Read more to discover the secrets and techniques of the covert emotional manipulators.

Covert Manipulation Techniques

You recognize precisely what covert emotional manipulation is, and is not, and the types of situations it can arise in. This is a great foundational understanding of the subject; however, it is also vital to apprehend some of the precise procedures used by manipulators of their pursuit of management. The whole cause of this sort of emotional manipulation is to keep it as undetected as possible. This section's goal is to blow this secret international wide open for all to recognize.

Love Bombing

Love bombing is a way typically utilized by emotional manipulators at the beginning of their interaction with a victim. It includes the acute, surprising, and forceful show of positive emotions towards a victim. This will seem counterproductive at the start. If a person is attempting to damage a person, why do they act excessively nice at first? As it only betters their targets ego.

The idea at the back of love bombing is it creates an intense feeling of belief, affection, and compliance from a victim to their manipulator. The quantity to which love bombing is used and the people its miles used on, relies upon the manipulator's evaluation of the situation. A victim who is lonely, determined, and in search of aid and comfort is possible to be love-bombed more intensely and openly because the manipulator feels they will be more receptive to it. Furthermore, an emotionally stable victim will require a less intense and toned-down messages of positive reassurance.

Two important lessons about CEM may be found out from the description of the love-bombing approach. First, it illustrates flawlessly the covert nature of CEM. Believe seeking to apprehend love bombing as something bad. "Properly, this character became sincerely first-class to me and made my experience surely top." This kind of declaration is not going to trigger any purple flags or warning signs and symptoms of abuse taking region. This is a textbook instance of how something with a poor outcome may be disguised as something fine.

The second standard lesson associated with CEM we can analyze from understanding love bombing is how CEM is calibrated to the specific scenario every target offers. Skilled manipulators will have covertly managed many people in their beyond and could have discovered from enjoying. They consequently realize the right intensity and timing of any given CEM approach in any given scenario.

As an example, each person responds differently to diverse "Loving" gestures, compliments paintings to name a few, while presents will have greater of an impact on others. If someone who used the knowledge provided within the discipline of CEM attempted to achieve a goal, it's far not going they would have a good deal of success in doing so. That is as it calls for the expertise of an appropriate extent to which a victim will respond to positive strategies and now not others. Just as a doctor can prescribe the proper remedy in the right dose, the skilled manipulator can use the right manipulation at the perfect time and the most ideal situation for a successful outcome.

Reinforcement - A CEM Stacked Collection

Intermittent fine reinforcement is a way that often follows love bombing chronologically. It is a way of controlling a victim without them understanding what's going on. The everyday collection of a textbook CEM situation involves love bombing followed by advantageous reinforcement of the ego and subtle reiteration of manipulative ideas. The motive for this series will now be made clear.

Love bombing is the unconditional, unearned, and intense display of positivity from a manipulator to their target within the earliest days of their interaction. It has the cause of softening up a sufferer's defenses, growing their reliance at the man or woman manipulating them and setting the frame of a high-quality dating, friendship, or any different form the interaction takes.

The next step after the love bombing is constant and perfectly timed positive reinforcement This is a switch of conduct wherein the manipulator moves forward with relentless, unconditional positivity in the direction of their victim. Alternatively, the manipulator withholds any positivity whatsoever until a time the victim is acting a preferred behavior, for instance, if the manipulator desires their sufferer to call them regularly, the manipulator will rarely show a positive response while this takes place. The victim might be unaware that positive reinforcement is getting used strategically in opposition to them; however, they will subconsciously observe the desires of the manipulator to reveal the most ideal response and emotional face to move forward with.

This predictable positive reinforcement is then changed by using periodic impactful positive reinforcement or PIPR. PIPR includes the withholding of expressions of positivity, even when desired behavior is displayed. As an example, if the manipulator wants their victim to buy them material things and the victim complies, the manipulator will praise this as positive behavior with exceptional emotional connection.

This unpredictability causes a deep, unconscious yearning for positive manipulators attention on behalf of the sufferer, without the victim ever having any knowledge of what's happening. The victim will then begin to chase the better and more positive response from the manipulator by any means viable. The manipulator has their sufferer behaving positively and the sufferer will haven't any conscious awareness about any aspect of what they are doing to them, let alone why they are doing it.

The preceding sequential approach of affection bombing, advantageous reinforcement, and eventually intermittent tremendous reinforcement illustrates one manner a covert emotional manipulator can installation high-quality expression and bloodless withdrawal to sculpt the emotional reaction of their victims. Reality denial is a CEM technique that starts with effects upon the thoughts, instead of feelings of the victim. On the other hand, the consequences can devastate a victim's emotions, as you are approximately to see.

Truth Denial

One of the most terrifying experiences a human can bear is the sensation of losing their sanity. That is horrific enough if it can be defined by way of something comprehensible, along with mental contamination or the temporary byproduct of social pressure but is even more unsettling if the feeling of insanity has been covertly triggered with the aid of an emotional manipulator.

Truth denial refers to quite a several CEM strategies that each one has an identical purpose—destroying a sufferer's sanity to serve the manipulator's own selfish goals. The approaches when reality denial takes its effect will now be explored in extra detail.

One of the important principles determining reality denial is graduality. Manipulators are not going to immediately goal for the overall destruction of a victim's sanity as such an outcome is sort of not possible to gain without being detected. Instead, experienced manipulators generally tend to take the "Slowly but surely" approach. This entails the sluggish erosion of a person's sanity until the belief of their colleges is standing on the flimsiest of foundations.

How does a covert manipulator start the method of eroding a victim's sanity? It starts regularly with the small-scale undermining of a victim's self-belief of their memory. The manipulator will engineer numerous situations wherein a victim is left overthinking their personal recollection of events. The manipulator will usually make certain that their very own portrayal of what took place is the only recollection that ends up the most credible.

This technique of sweet sixteen self-assurance erosion serves covertly manipulative functions concurrently. First, it reduces the sufferer consider in their powers to keep in mind and knowledge. Second, this trust is transferred onto the manipulator instead. It is critical to note that this will by no means look like a massive deal at the beginning. The manipulator will come across as sincere because of the individual with slightly better memory. The victim may also be grateful they have a person whose recollection they could depend upon!

Over time, the covert emotional manipulator will add to the severity of the occasions they make the sufferer query. What begins as seemingly innocent and insignificant event might be amplified right into a victim losing all self-belief in their very own recollective strength. The most insidious detail of this procedure is the victim's tendency to blame their very own mind for the loss of potential. Professional manipulators may also be those pulling the strings, but by no means, ever letting the sufferer grow to be privy to what is taking place.

CHAPTER 2
WHAT'S DARK PSYCHOLOGY TRIAD

What is the Dark Triad? - Expertise the Unholy Trinity

The Dark Triad is the important thing idea that ties collectively every other thing of dark psychology. The name seems like something from a movie, however, it's a longstanding legitimate psychological idea recognized by way of all the top practitioners in the field. The dark Triad is not anything extra than the identity of the three maximum detrimental and harmful psychological character traits a person will have. This chapter will explain in detail what every one of those developments is and the specific approaches they come upon in exercise. You're positive to recognize that the Dark Triad is the source from which all different dark psychology stems.

What are the 3 trends that form the Triad? Machiavellianism, psychopathy, and narcissism. Many people may additionally listen to those terms and suppose they judge them instinctively. A psychopath is a risky assassin, right? Does a narcissist take too many selfies? Incorrect. Understanding is strength. Each of the ideas should be reputable and understood for their strength to come to be obvious.

To assist your know-how of the powerful Triad, an outline of each of its additives, and what they consist of, will first be furnished. Examples of how every Dark psychology trait manifest in actual-world conditions will then be explored. This chapter gives a comprehensive perception of the theory and the practice of the three most massive and damaging standards in the international of dark psychology.

What's Machiavellianism?

Machiavellianism draws its call from the political logician Machiavelli. In his conventional work on political energy and have an impact on, "The Prince," Machiavelli outlines thoughts, concepts, and tactics that have served as a blueprint for seekers of having an impact on at some stage in records. So how exactly does a Machiavellian individual stumble upon?

The hallmarks of this dark Triad trait are always a willingness to focus on self-interest, information on the importance of picture, perception and superficial look, and the ruthless exercising of strength and cruelty over compassion and mercy.

In simple terms, Machiavellian people are tremendously strategic of their technique to lifestyles. The ramifications and consequences of any given movement are a concept out and assessed in phrases of the way they'll impact upon the man or woman carrying them out. The Machiavellian technique to the sector may be summed up in a single query: "How will this action benefit me, and the way will my public perception be impacted as a result?"

In addition, Machiavellian people are masters of doing something, in my opinion, that serves them at the same time as still dealing with to preserve a high-quality public image. However, to take one instance, consider former President Invoice Clinton. He managed to behave in step with his sexual desires while nonetheless last "Liked" amongst the general public. Contrast this with many other politicians who've succumbed to more-marital temptation and are vilified in the public eye as a result.

Some other instance from the political area is the public photograph of Barack Obama vs. that of George W. Bush. Ask around and most of the people will explain that Bush becomes a conflicted president and Obama a president of peace. In real fact, they're each about as militant as each other. Obama managed to govern his public notion to serve his photograph at the same time as Bush did not. That is an effective lesson on the idea of belief vs. fact.

What Is Psychopathy?

Psychopathy is hard to precisely outline, but it refers to a mental condition concerning superficial appeal, impulsivity, and a loss of normally held "Human" feelings inclusive of empathy and regret. A person who is famous enough of these tendencies, referred to as a psychopath. Psychopaths are several of the riskiest humans to walk the planet and are examples of wolves in sheep's clothing.

People would possibly associate the phrase "Psychopath" with the photo of a machete-wielding mad man sporting a mask. The truth is terrifying. Proper psychopaths are more likely to be the handsome, captivating stranger who wins their sufferers over earlier than ruining or maybe ending their existence.

Interestingly, some of the top names are in the discipline of business consistently rating extraordinarily on psychopathy persona assessments. Many people are beginning to see psychopathy as more of a trouble for society than for the psychopaths' own lives. Psychopaths are often capable of getting to the top in any discipline they pick, be it finance or serial homicide, due to the fact they are now not constrained by forcefully employing the compassionate indecision that most people enjoy.

What's Narcissism?

A whole lot of human beings think of narcissism and the narcissists who own this trait, as folks who honestly "Love Themselves." This is on the right track but not precise enough while expertise narcissism via the lens of the triad. It is miles feasible to have self-love without being a narcissist. What are several the distinctions among a person with high shallowness and someone narcissistic to an extent that they're considered on the spectrum for The Dark Triad?

A person who meets the scientific diagnostic criteria for narcissism, to the point that they've taken into consideration to have a psychological sickness, is likely to exhibit a number the subsequent personality markers continually. Narcissists are likely to have an overly inflated self-confidence, including seeing their existence as special and one of the most important in history. Narcissists are not, in their minds, only special—they are advanced. They are a higher species of person, better in repute than "Every day" human beings. Their conduct reflects their feeling of self-confidence.

Some of the commonplace outward manifestations of narcissism are a lack of ability to accept criticism or dissent in any manner. Just like this need to be agreed with, is the need to be flattered. Narcissists require constant praise, approval, and reputation and tend to organize their lives in a way that offers them regularly to get admission to others who fulfill this need.

The Dark Triad Carried Out

You now apprehend the idea of the Triad and the three psychological trends that shape the basis of this fundamental area of psychology. It's far more important to no longer apprehend the Triad itself, however, the various approaches where it manifests in actual conduct. A few examples of behaviors will now be supplied for each of the 3 Triad regions.

Machiavellian Moves

You understand that a Machiavellian character is a political schemer involved as a great deal with their public photo as they are with their bloodless-hearted pursuit of self-interest chiefly else. How do Machiavellian people behave? This may be a hard aspect to apprehend as Machiavellian people are, employing their nature, adept at hiding their true intentions and moves from public scrutiny. The following behaviors are all conventional Machiavellian techniques that you are probably to come upon at one time or every other.

For the general public who do not meet the clinical definition of Machiavellianism, their public persona is often a reflection of their true, non-public self. Anyone polishes their appearance and behavior a little in public, but employing and huge, most of the people's outward photograph is not anything extra than a refined portrayal of who they truly are.

Besides, Machiavellian people have a clear difference between what they may be and how they come across inside the public eye. Examples assist to illustrate this idea. There are numerous instances of serial murderers who have gotten away with their crimes for a long time because their outward photograph is to unrealistically different from what humans imagine a murderer to be. An example is a non-secular leader who spends a whole lot of time on charity paintings and seeming to help ordinary people whilst surely committing horrific acts of violence and sexual attack in their spare time. Their public movements are the "Mask" that hides their private self from scrutiny for the sort of long term.

Examples of one of these distinctions among motive and look can be observed in regions much less severe than serial homicide. There are endless stories of leaders inside the international of commercial enterprises who manage to ruthlessly reduce jobs and pursue profit over people every time viable. The very nice of these bosses, in phrases of Machiavellianism, is without a doubt capable of getting humans to buy into the belief that they are behaving through necessity or maybe compassion! Such leaders are nearly role models for folks that desire to serve simplest their dreams while seeming to be a "Man of the human beings" on the equal time.

A willingness to take advantage of humans is another hallmark of Machiavellian individuals. To demonstrate this example, consider a newcomer to a hostile workplace. If this man or woman became no longer clinically Machiavellian, they would look around and notice a room full of various coworkers to get to know. Each human being is much like them, some good people and some awful people.

A Machiavellian workplace newcomer would see every single colleague, boss, or team member as only a useful resource or piece of a puzzle to use and take advantage of. As opposed to seeing others as fellow human beings, the Machiavellian individual might simply see a series of strategic threats and weaknesses to manage, take advantage of, or neutralize. That is a huge part of the cause that Machiavellian humans are so aware of how they come across. They recognize this outward portrayal is the key to exerting influence and efficaciously exploiting anybody they stumble upon.

One of the authentic Machiavellian ideas, derived from "The Prince," is an insistence on only preserving a phrase or promise if it serves self-hobby to achieve this. At the beginning, this concept may lead to knowledge of Machiavellian people as folks that are known as untrustworthy. This is a misunderstanding. If a Machiavellian character breaks character, they do so in a manner that simply makes them seem noble and one way or the other praiseworthy. This will be illustrated with an example drawn from cutting-edge politics. Do you recall, back to Barack Obama's election, his promise to shut down Guantanamo Bay? Has this been saved? No. Alternatively, Obama by some means has portrayed himself as a "Nobleman held returned via a merciless device" in place of a "Politician who broke his phrase." This is the fundamental distinction between a skilled Machiavellian guy and a normal person who can't be relied on.

The instilling of worry in the humans around them is another hallmark of Machiavellian individuals. This stems directly from "The Prince," which urges human beings to be both feared and loved concurrently. If this isn't always possible, then the eBook states being feared is leading to being loved. This concept of the desirability of being loved and feared at the same time relates at once to the Machiavellian trait of splitting a public and personal perception. The appropriate Machiavellian is capable of encouraging fear and obedience in the very individuals who would claim to feel love more potent than fear as a result.

Psychopathic Actions

You have got clear information about the primary psychopathic tendencies and what differentiates actual psychopaths from the ones inside the public imagining. Until you are an educated psychotherapist with intimate access to a person, you'll no longer be capable of recognizing them as a psychopath on the premise of theoretical expertise. Alternatively, it is vital to apprehend the outward manifestations of psychopathy, as those are generally the best manner to stumble on psychopathy behavior earlier than it is far too late.

Physical attraction is one of the most commonplace outward behaviors of a psychopathic character. It needs to be understood, but that is purely superficial charm instead of deep, genuine allure. If you reflect on a charming person from your personal life you are likely to realize that they had fantastic personality developments undermining outward displays of conduct. If this type of clearly captivating man or woman behaved in a captivating manner was an actual expression of kindness and a preference to make human beings happy. This isn't the case with a psychopath.

Psychopaths can show all the outward symptoms of appeal such as bodily elegance, obvious friendly personality and interest in others. The inward motivation behind such outward shows is the reason it is this kind of red flag. Psychopaths view charm as very a good deal part of an equation.

Mendacity is any other trademark feature of psychopaths. It is not, on its very own, enough to classify a person within the diagnostic class of psychopathy. While combined with other tendencies, however, it can imply a psychopathic persona. Lying comes as naturally for a psychopath as breathing does for people with extreme mental stability. A psychopath can convincingly conceal the fact as something they want it to be in a specific moment. Psychopaths also don't show outward signs and symptoms of a liar as they haven't any emotional attachment or emotions of disgrace, guilt, or excitement about their lies. For psychopaths, mendacity is simply "Doing what is wanted at the time."

A loss of regret is some other distinctive feature that separates psychopaths from non-psychopathic individuals. Many human beings who've committed atrocious acts, which include homicide, experience a deep sense of guilt and shame about what they have performed or even take their own life because of those emotions. It's not that psychopaths take longer to be remorseful—they're physically incapable of it. Asking a psychopath to feel regret is like asking a deaf person to concentrate on song lyrics.

Directly related to a lack of regret is a lack of guilt. People usually feel a sense guilt after they have damaged a few types of ethical norms that they personally feel. As psychopaths do not think in terms of proper and wrong, instead in beneficial or no longer beneficial, guilt is an unheard-of concept to them. The closest reason a psychopath may proceed to guilt or cause regret; is under the belief that they did not carry out their psychopathic deeds to their personally acceptable standard.

A loss of impulse control is another signature aspect of psychopathy. Most people have inner controls and mechanisms that prevent them from behaving rashly. A psychopath lacks these prevention mechanisms. If a psychopath sees an opportunity they want to take advantage of, they will act without hesitation or the 2nd concept. This may contain killing a person they wish to kill, raping a person they want to rape, or stealing something they desire to have. This ruthless impulsivity is what makes psychopaths some of the trickiest people in fields consisting of the army and world of business. The automatic response to take decisive action is a trait many non-psychopaths lacks, and this lack honestly is a detriment to progress in lifestyles.

Empathy is a human capability to understand and share feelings on behalf of another. Psychopaths are utterly incapable of empathy of any kind. People unlike themselves do not register as real or worth anything at all to psychopaths. They are akin to stick figures crudely drawn on paper. Their lives do not have any value or any means outside of what they can offer to the psychopathic man or woman. If a psychopath sees something awful happen to someone their response is to speculate, "How does this affect me? How am I able to use this to my gain?" in place of any type of heartfelt response in any respect.

Narcissistic Actions

One of the earliest signs and symptoms of a narcissist is fantasies and imaginings of vast ranges of strength and status. Many narcissists file formative year's fantasies of being worshipped and adored. At the same time as many non-narcissistic people might also have the occasional daydream of power and status, a narcissist will ignorantly assume they deserve this reward and elevation as a fundamental right. The truth they're no longer being worshipped and respected always, is a personal attack to the mental outlook of a psychopath.

The conscious though that "I'm better than a quite number of the people, they are no longer worthy of me, and I am better than them" is a common viewpoint of major narcissists. The general public experience fluctuations in self-worth or pride due to their achievements and behaviors in life. This isn't always the case with narcissists. Narcissists view flattery and reward as something that they need to automatically get hold of always, regardless of any alternatives on occasions.

The inflated sense of self-confidence that narcissists experience internally has implications on their outward behavior, this generally manifests in methods—the need for agreement, praise, and the hatred of complaint or rejection. Reward and settlement are like oxygen for the narcissistic ego while complaints and dissent are like poison.

To recognize what narcissism seems like when taken to its logical conclusion, picture a dictator in an isolated nation. Such humans demand worship from those they have strength over, the building of statues in their likeness and whole obedience and reputation. Any act of dissent or confrontation is met with speedy and brutal punishment. North Korea might be an excellent modern-day instance of the acute manifestation of narcissism. The rulers of that country demand to be respected like Gods and execute and torture all people who even dares to question an idea or concept which isn't completely in step with the dictatorship's personal doctrine.

Sadism

Sadism is a surprising, but vital footnote to the Triad chapter. Present-day psychological researchers have proposed that the dark triad is, in actual truth, a dark tetrad with sadistic persona ailment providing the fourth pillar. Sadism is possibly the hardest character trait to understand as its miles the least relatable for plenty of human beings.

Nearly all and sundry have an issue of their personality or background, wherein they can apprehend signs of Machiavellianism, psychopathy, and narcissism to an extent. Sadism is alien to most people though as they can't even rationally apprehend the basis for it.

Sadism is defined because of the deriving of delight from the suffering of others. This provides a worrying size to the preexisting Triad developments. If, as an example, a Machiavellian leader triggered other individuals to suffer, they could not regret it, but would additionally not enjoy the suffering. It would be viewed disapprovingly. Upload sadism into the mixture, but the traumatic incidence of pride, even sexual delight, being derived from brutal acts occurs.

The defining characteristic that sets sadism apart from other aspects of dark psychology is the reality of it, it entails cruelty for no purpose aside from satisfaction. It isn't to serve a bigger aim or due to a few inherent acts of manipulating. Sadists are searching for out the suffering of others only for leisure, in an equal way ordinary people would possibly watch a sports contest.

CHAPTER 3

DARK PSYCHOLOGY PROCESSES

Psychological Approaches to Manipulation

How do you get what you need?

Take a minute to consider a current situation in which you wanted something from any other man or woman. Perhaps you wanted your accomplice to wash the dishes, or you wanted a promotion out of your boss, or you desired a person at a party to go on a date with you. How did you get it?

In a perfect world, we may also want to ask for all the subjects we want from people and they would comply without questions. On the other hand, the world isn't the best and we will get the entirety of outcomes that we want on a first try. What are you capable of doing to get what you need?

There are a variety of sincere, moral answers to this query. However, there are also unethical solutions. If you try to get what you want through deception, lies, or indirect approaches, you're using the act of manipulation.

We will go over the eleven tactics of manipulation. We aren't providing you with this equipment so you can leave and control others. Think of this as a warning. People are looking to manipulate others every day. If you could spot the signs of manipulation, you may see via them and be selective over the friends you keep and your relationship with others.

The 11 Techniques of Manipulation

Charm

We all know someone who makes use of a wink and praise to get what they want. Human beings need to sense attractive and desired. Manipulators play into these feelings by being charming. They consider that once a person starts to get a little flirty, they'll start to be attracted to the manipulator and could be more likely to follow what the manipulator's wants.

Coercion

This tactic isn't all a laugh and flirty while someone is "Coercing" another to do something, they will be using fear of damage or threats. They might say, "In case you don't help me rob this financial institution, I'll kick your dog." Yikes! The individual being coerced may feel as although the outcomes of not doing the request are worse than the outcomes of doing the act.

Silent Remedy

Silence is an incredibly powerful manipulation and negotiation device. It makes us traumatic; if someone is silent or refusing to talk, we may additionally sense the urge to give into their desires or give them something they need just to interrupt the silence.

Reason

Not all manipulation tactics are unethical; however, they can be used unethically. The cause is a notable example of the sort of manipulation tactic. People may additionally use causes or logical arguments to get what they want. They'll inform someone (or themselves) something like, "If you help me to rob this bank, you may be capable of feeding your family," nothing wrong with that, right? However, while it's tough to argue in opposition to a person who uses purpose as a manipulation tactic, you will be more likely to break down and supply the manipulator that they need.

Regression

When people interact with each different adults, it may be smooth for everyone to maintain their ground. Although one person reverts to appearing like a toddler, things may go haywire, that is the regression tactic; someone may also whine, cry, or pout till they get their way. Humans may give in without a doubt due to the fact they want the infantile conduct to stop.

Self-Abasement

Now not all manipulation strategies contain insulting or forcing the alternative man or woman to do something. If a manipulator makes use of self-abasement to get what they want, they will humble themselves. Self-abasement can be used while a manipulator wishes someone to forgive them, agree with them, or make other efforts to strengthen a relationship.

Responsibility Invocation

Let us say you have considered getting your nails done. It's easy to simply decide, "No, I'm no longer going to get my nails done." In case you already booked an appointment, but it's not so smooth to just wait it out and not get your nails achieved. Responsibility invocation uses these types of duties to convince someone to follow through with plans. A manipulator might say, "However, you promised…" or "I've already booked the reservations…" to make pronouncing "No" a lot harder.

Hardball

Hardball procedures take coercion to the subsequent level. At the same time as a person may additionally use coercion to threaten them with the fear of harm, hardball techniques truly motive damage or physical injury.

Satisfaction Induction

For lots, pleasure induction is an innocent manipulation tactic. When a person invokes the delight induction tactic, they are truly telling a person that the motion will be amusing and that the individual will enjoy it. "Come on, it will be amusing!"

Social Evaluation

The Social assessment concept describes how we present ourselves to others. Many people measure their achievement, attractiveness, and presence of personality trends through the evaluation of others. Manipulators realize this tendency more prominently. They will use social comparison to move or persuade people to take the next action. "Your friend at your workplace does this for her accomplice." "The celeb within the mag in on X weight-reduction plan...You should be too."

Financial Reward

Manipulators may play into a person's greed by imparting them money to commit acts that they normally wouldn't commit. In case you have been offered 1,000,000 bucks, would you commit a criminal offense?

Who're master Manipulators?

Let's boil down some stereotypes here. Ladies are regularly framed as master manipulators. This just isn't genuine. There are no differences in techniques of manipulation based on gender - studies show that ladies and men equally carry out those strategies. Just watch any "Pick-up artist" paintings his "Magic" on YouTube, and the myths of women being manipulators will disappear before your eyes.

How do approaches of Manipulation show up in the

big five?

Manipulation tactics show up often within the Prince. Machiavelli is one of the international's most famous manipulators. He's so infamous that one of the Dark Triad persona developments is named after him.

People who are more "Machiavellian" are much more likely to use (and justify their use of) manipulation tactics. They accept the truth to be that they are above ethical actions and deserve to get whatever they want, even supposing they get it by manipulation. This connection is alternatively obvious, but they're also are some connections between techniques of manipulation and the large 5 persona developments, let's take a look at them.

If you'd like to see what your character rankings are, you can take my loose persona quiz; however, it doesn't component those processes of manipulation into your results.

Extraversion

Folks that rating excessive in extraversion are more likely to apply coercion and duty invocation.

Agreeableness

Individuals who were rating high in agreeableness are much more likely to apply satisfaction induction and motive to get what they need. These manipulation techniques are some of the most ethical; they convince people that they'll get something fantastic out of taking certain actions. Conversely, people who are more unpleasant are much more likely to are seeking for revenge on humans by coercion and the silent treatment.

Conscientiousness

Just like agreeableness, those who are rated high on faithfulness are more likely to select purpose over different manipulation procedures. Folks who score low in conscientiousness are more likely to pick methods that can be probably criminal offenses like coercion or illegal types of financial praise.

Openness

Individuals who score high in openness are more likely to apply motive and now and then delight induction or obligation invocation. Successful reasoning frequently calls for better information on logic or higher intelligence.

High openness and high intellect are generally related. Conversely, those who score low in openness are more likely to use social assessment as manipulation.

As you examine relationships in your life, keep an eye out for master manipulators and signs of the subsequent manipulation techniques. The more you know about manipulation, the less difficult it'll be to see those strategies at gatherings and gain extra control over the choices you're making.

Seven Mental Persuasion Tips – How to influence a person's hints?

Why do you make the decisions you make or does it matters that you do? There's usually a cause and psychologists are gaining knowledge that many of our movements are motivated in ways we don't understand and that these effects can mean a whole range of things. Even moderate persuasion could have a big impact on us. In the pursuit of your goals, you may discover which you want to convince humans to invest money into you or to cooperate with you. Likewise, for one purpose or another, you may need a person to see your side of things. In those times, lots of separate similar ones, knowing how to take the benefit of psychology to influence others can be a useful tool.

On the other hand, it's vital to be responsible and respectful when you need to sway someone. Persuasion isn't always the same as manipulation. Persuasion is executed with proper intentions to reveal someone your intentions and with any luck getting them to pick to comply or believe you. Manipulation is done with ill reason and commonly includes deceit or tricks to persuade someone to agree or comply. In case you're not telling the entire tale or are distorting the truth to convince humans to do something to benefit you, however, it will be complicated for them, that is manipulation. Nudging people to see your point of view so that they're willing to trust you, it is persuasion. Persuasion isn't forceful, it isn't misleading, and it isn't harmful to the individuals being persuaded. Keep this in mind when implementing the subsequent reasons for your existence.

1. Last Phrases

A few select phrases are more convincing than others. Words called "Last Phrases" may be included in your argument or point to move more precisely. They're grouped into three categories: God terms, Satan phrases, and charismatic terms. God phrases are also referred to as power phrases and tend to be advantageous and appealing. For example, when you are talking about protection, some associated god phrases are "Assuring" and "Confirmed." Alternatively, devil words are more terrible and repulsive to audiences. Following that logic, a pair that may be used are "Risky" and "Risky." Next, there are charismatic terms that are a little trickier; they're typically abstract, however, appealing due to historical context—phrases like "Freedom" or "Development." Any of the words in these classes can change the manner people think and feel about an idea or viewpoint. They prompt specific reactions because we've been programmed through experience over the course of our lives to understand these phrases completely. You may use those varieties of words to create appeal and draw someone in or to make an option to switch appear very undesirable.

2. Talk Quick

The delivery of the words you've selected also affects humans' responses to them while you talk quickly, it aids in persuasion for a couple of reasons. First, speaking fast means that the individual listening must absorb what you're saying quite quickly to hold up with you. It offers them time to hear you, however, make it tougher for them to nitpick your argument. Nevertheless, they'll see predominant issues if there are any. However, they'll be too busy listening and processing what they agree with to stop you in order to choose a viewpoint within the information given. Speaking quickly also can make you appear more confident. Talking slowly and fumbling for the proper word can truly harm your pitch, but while you could communicate easily at an especially brief pace—but not so fast that you're hard to recognize or follow—the people listening perceive you as assured and knowledgeable, consciously, or subconsciously. If they see you as having these tendencies, they're much more likely to need to get onto your side, even if they don't realize precisely why you appeal to them.

3. The Proper Frame Language

Together with your phrases, your body speaks volumes like speaking fast, the people you're talking to might also notice your stance and moves consciously, but they might just take your word subconsciously to impact their opinion of you in a diffused way. Rise up, shoulders lower back, and secure. Don't fiddle with your hands, however, do use hand gestures now and then to emphasize your enthusiasm. Don't look down on the floor or at notes; instead, make eye contact: however, don't keep it so frequent with an unmarried person that it becomes unsettling. Searching assured tells people non-verbally which you recognize what you're doing and recognize what you're talking about. It'll go away an impression that makes people want to aid you in your further ventures and makes them more probably to take you more seriously in an argument.

4. Repetition

Have you ever listened to music for the first time and not appreciated it, simplest to return to loving it later after listening to it numerous extra times? The human mind loves repetition and styles, so whilst we're uncovered to a concept time. Again, we can come to adore it greater or receive it more without difficulty than while we first heard it. Although, you're pitching a plan or concept, repeat the crucial facts two or three times. For instance, if you need to convince someone of a product's high-quality, repeat its efficiency stats as compared to different comparable products. In case you're in a casual argument with a friend or colleague, repeat a concept in specific approaches at some stage in your argument. They will no longer understand, they simply heard the same element extra than as soon as. However, their mind will take be aware and they're more likely to start to see your opinion. On this sort of state of affairs it's properly to break it down into three instances; if it's glaringly the identical information repeated more than one instances—instead of being subtly transformed with the equal core idea, it can without a doubt have the opposite effect and leave the man or woman feeling more evidence to argue against it.

5. Balanced Arguments

Very few ideas are perfect; even the first-rate plans, standards, and views can have a flaw or two. Even as you may think the quality manner to steer a person is to consciously reassure the positives and attempt to cowl up all potential Darks, studies have virtually proven that humans reply excellent to well-balanced arguments. Although, many people while being pitched a concept, will search for the holes in it; in case you don't acknowledge obvious wrongs in the viewpoint, they may see you as deceitful. Or, if they don't note the flaws, but do believe that your concept is too good to be real, they're probably to have a hard believing you and might be hard to control. Again, studies have found one-sided arguments to be more a hit in persuasion, probably because your honest about the much less than ideal point of view, your concept makes you appear straightforward. People are drawn to those they sense they can believe and are more likely to pay attention to you in case you come off that manner.

6. Inform A Story rather Than Reporting Statistics

Human beings reply to personal interactions. Have a look at Carnegie Mellon College in comparison efficacy of two exclusive pitch patterns. In each, students have been trying to collect donations to enhance the lives of people in various African nations experiencing drought, meal shortages, and dislocation from their houses. One pitch becomes centered on statistics and numbers to explain how terrible the situation became. Although, the alternative pitch informed the story of a ravenous female named Rokia and included a photo of her. The scholars who used the tale raised extra than twice as lots of cash for the purpose. The realization became that facts are impersonal and might leave people feeling disconnected from the idea whilst making matters private makes people want to get involved. You don't have to tell a story near a person, actual or imagined; you can also provide an explanation for someone how your idea impacts their life on a private degree. Any way you can reach the individual you're attempting to influence privately is useful.

7. Taking Some Power Away From The Powerful

Although offering a concept to a person with greater social power than you like your boss, a successful commercial enterprise character, or a leader of some type—being capable of taking a portion of their power away can help to influence them to see your way of things. This might sound a tad sinister. However, it's no longer the truth. The entire concept is that many people with charisma recognize that they're unique and generally tend to look down on people who are of a lesser position. On the other hand, you can take some of their energy through exposing them to things which might be new to them; show them that you're more knowledgeable than them in the subject you're speaking about by providing information that they are not likely to know. In case you're the more knowledgeable within the scenario, they'll make sense less effectively. Then, closer to the end of the conversation, remind them in their position of power to lead them to feel extra confident in their evaluation of your pitch. It's a tremendous approach for leaders of many kinds but may be beneficial in arguments with folks who simply experience common superiority too.

There are many situations when persuasion is a precious talent. Understanding strategies that influence your target demographic on a psychological level will help you convince more consistently.

How to Haggle – 8 Exceptional Psychological Negotiation Strategies And Strategies

Many people are hesitant to haggle more, but the credit score emergency implies lots of us might also want to discover new recommendations while trying to haggle for our cash and underneath are the top eight suggestions to haggle better.

1. Do Your Research

Start with the aid of asking a vital question: How much ideally would you like to spend on this product? If you have set your monetary plan, your goal is to reach a deal that gives a perfect service or product for a fixed quantity you plan to spend. The next step is to research the item you want to shop for. All objects have their unusual personal appeal. However, what do you truly require from the object? There's no purpose for paying for extra additives you will never use. Look around and discover the object you believe, you studied will best healthy your necessities and spending plan. Look at eBay, Amazon, Craigslist, and different online marketplaces for the best deals. Find out the amount you should purchase from a series of references and make the best decision. If you're buying it domestically and with a person, you could barter with, in addition, we will circulate directly to the following steps. If the object is online and the rate is non-negotiable, you then might want to close this video.

2. Build A Rapport With The Salesperson

Therefore, what's the major aspect you must do when you meet the salesperson? Grin and ask their first name.

Use it as regularly as you could inside the dialogue. Provide them your call too. It is beautiful how a fundamental trick like that may start to separate obstructions. A few good visits before you start speaking to workers providing a service or is a step in the right direction. In case you're stuck for an idea, without a doubt, communicate approximately the climate, or test out my different theories on common situations. It doesn't make a difference what you speak about; the length is determined by how smooth it is to break the ice. Have some downtime and develop a friendship if possible; however, remember why you're there to score a super deal. Psychologically, if you can get the salesclerk to have an unconscious bias towards you, they'll be a good deal more forced to present you a better deal.

3. Wait, Don't Haggle Too Soon

Patience is essential in haggling or bartering. Try to not be in such a hurry to close a deal. Try to avoid even saying the cost in the first five mins. Allow the salesclerk to sink into the dialogue and you. It's generally amazing to provide the salesperson a hazard to tell you concerning the item you need to buy. Let them educate you about the product you're shopping for and play dumb when you must. You can realize a great deal now from the research you've completed, but for them, it's pleasant to listen to the statistics you're being given. Give them a chance to demonstrate to you the inventory on offer. They may have the audacity to provide a markdown on a product since it lacks the most recent trending features. Additionally, be looking for flaws, as we will talk this in a subsequent step.

4. Stand Your Ground

Dialogue and conversation offer you the chance to discover more about the man or woman you're handling. If they try to make a deal immediately and abruptly. You will have the experience of them attempting to steamroll you right into a sale, make certain they don't get away with it. Maintain your patience and stall them by asking questions to lessen their ability to make you impulsively buy a product. Understand how a shop clerk thinks about what they are attempting to influence you into buying. Perhaps they're hiding something. Being raced into setting apart with your money is horrible news and can cause consumers to regret it.

5. Let's Communicate Numbers

Never, ever let them recognize how high and low you are willing to pay. Giving that information away can hinder a bargain before it has even started and isn't haggling in any respect. You would be making the decision to no longer pay the maximum amount, so don't announce it. Strive not to mention and I don't anticipate you can thump any cash off? Do say I really like the ones get the value down and I'll purchase them nowadays. Try not to say I don't expect you can offer me a discount? Do say – What kind of deal can you offer me today? Be sure and focused. To get the first-rate deal, you ought to pass in so low it's verging on traumatic. If something cost them $100 to buy and you may buy them for $50 on eBay, attempt providing $20. Of course, they'll most likely say no, however, if they say yes to a higher charge, you'll spend the rest of your day wondering if you could have gotten it for a lower price . Now you have got as a base minimum sale price.

Although you suggest a bargain, don't communicate your intentions again until the salesperson brings it up themselves. In case you say too much, you will sound stressed, as though you are attempting to justify the offer you have made. Many people get nervous, try and fill the space; it takes the sales associate to disperse with the useless chatter. While you make your offer, gesture your head marginally as you do it. Also, keep your body language open and pleasant, hold your feet pointed towards them, cast off any obstacles among you two, and shake arms assembly them while preserving your wrist open towards them.

6. Have An "Get Out Of Jail Free" Card

One factor you must have while you move into any commercial enterprise circumstance is a get out of jail free card. I imply a motive to get away the store if you discover the burden is getting a piece too first-rate, otherwise you find out a huge flaw inside the product. Have an excuse ready; something that salesclerk can't make you stay longer with. As an example, I have a dental appointment in 10 minutes. I cannot stay any longer. I must carry the kids up from faculty; my extensive other/wife/companion is unwell. I will communicate with them about this until they're higher. It's going to take the warm temperature off if the weight of your bargaining receives an excessive amount of; also, you want an easy out.

7. Extras

My recommendation is to dependably ask for more than the original on any deal you make. Earlier than you begin speaking to the commercial enterprise body of workers, have a look at around the shop or showroom for extras you may want to get for nothing like a major factor of your deal. Make certain your options to add is well thought out. You're now not susceptible to persuade the shop clerk to toss inexpensive matters as extras. However, they'll nicely contain some free assistants to run with the item you are buying in case you let them know it will wrap the whole thing up. An ideal opportunity to elevate the subject is the point that you have haggled strongly. Also, you sense past doubt the salesperson gained drop any extra on price.

Recognize which extras to ask for when the time dawns on that last push. Try no longer to do it in the beginning of an engagement as the provider will comprise that freebie with the final value that isn't always an additional in any manner. Maybe while you get near a charge, the seller needs. However, you believe you studied it's too excessive, recommend including are greater to simply accept his present-day charge and preserve with tip quantity 8.

8. Clinching The Deal

No salesclerk will toss you of the store out for requesting markdown, so long as you do it in a respectful and gracious manner. Deals are there to be executed, specifically in an emergency. In case you see someone wanting money on a Craigslist advert or Facebook submit, you're at an advantage. Make sure you shake the vendor's hand and thank them for the purchase. While you get that better than the common deal, the feeling of fulfillment you sense isn't always pretty much the cash you've spared. It's far likewise about demonstrating something to yourself. You've set yourself a look at and come by like a champ. It's noteworthy support and every time you exchange for merchandise in a shop or showroom in the future, your information will increase consistently. The more you do it, the better you get. That is the way it works.

Seven Psychological Cash Saving Hints – How to save

extra money each month?

Getting to know the way to save money can be hard if you weren't taught any money saving habits when you were young. Spending money is a vital thing that is inlaid with how our thoughts work and knowing the psychology tricks at the back of this puts you ahead in the money-saving goal. I'm going to provide you seven psychological tricks you can follow on your day to day life to save more money every month. While you go out to eat somewhere, buy groceries, or simply to buy things, attempt to use exact change rather than a debit card or check. Although using coins, you have an emotional attachment to the physical fabric paper. I also propose setting up a financial savings account and having as a minimum of 5% of your earnings go directly to that account.

"If you couldn't degree it, you can't manage it" turned into stated by the well-known Peter Drucker, and it's real. I created a month-to-month balance sheet for around six months in the past. It's the first-rate to peer where your money goes once you begin saving it. Developing finances and sticking to it can be difficult as first;

however, as you practice and live frugally that financial institutions savings account will continue to grow every month.

1) Coins

This is a big one while you go out to explore someplace new, buy groceries, or just to buy things, attempt to use cold hard cash rather than a debit card or credit. When using change, you have an emotional attachment to the physical material money, it's certainly more painful to hand a few cashiers $20 invoice than it's far to swipe a card, clearly because it appears like you're giving less whilst you swipe a card. Try to preserve change on you and limit that swiping. Bonus points in case you only convey a hundreds with you. Who's going to interrupt an easy crisp $100 bill for a few fuel station candy or milk on the grocery shop? I certainly I wouldn't.

2) Computerized Deductions

This is an exquisite tip due to the fact you may set it as much as now, not even understand the money is being got rid of. Wherever you work, maximum places have the option to take a percent or a positive amount out of your paycheck and to deposit it into a separate account. Try this and ship the cash instantly to a savings account you cannot make a withdrawal from. After a few years, and sure, becoming rich does take time. If there's a hobby, you'll have a ton of cost from that easy $100 a month going right into a savings account.

3) Month-to-month Assertion

"If you couldn't degree it, you can't manage it," turned into stated with the aid of the famous Peter Drucker, and it's true. I started a monthly balance sheet around six months ago, and it's superb to see in which your money goes once you begin dealing with it. I spend way less cash on little such things as meals and small gifts than I concept I did. Here's how I do it that I advocate you attempt it too. I write expenses on the pinnacle and upload in my month-to-month payments like smartphone invoice, hire, video scribe, automated savings deductions, mortgage fee, and different private things I pay together with the date they are deducted.

Underneath that, I depart the area for additional unpredictable things like gas, fast food, or even stuff like film leases and garments. Right under that I write my income, this is often quite a small space when you consider that I don't have very many earnings sources in the meantime. On the cease of the month, you add up overall costs, profits, and upload up your month-to-month profit or deficit. It facilitates knowing that in case you spend $8 on a few meals that you'll write it down and that little things upload up. Attempt it and it will help.

4) Avoid Advertising and Marketing

This is kind of a passive tip to keep money but attempt to avoid targeted advertising and marketing. This may lessen your probability of impulse buying stuff like an extra piece of gum on the cashier stand or that fantastic, brilliant coffee cup that doesn't tip over you watched you want. Lowering exposure to this type of content material will lessen what you think you need.

5) Now vs. Later

Have you ever idea you had been notably hungry sooner or later to your life? I wager if you drank a pitcher of cold water and waited 5 minutes, your transient hunger feeling will subside. It's exceptionally smooth to trick our minds; we want something NOW! It takes exercise to cultivate delayed gratification. You may do the identical precept as meals with your cash. As a substitute for buying that brilliant cool tech toy, wait a month, and the spot I case you, nonetheless, need it as awful. Possibilities are something new will come out, that's better or a few different regions you'll notice to be able to be a higher investment. Try and delay the things you spend your cash on. Also, you'll word extra money for your bank account every month!

6) Costs Into Hours

What I mean by way of this is to psychologically trick yourself into changing that $50 blouse into what number of hours you'll work for it. Would you visit paintings for five hours for that blouse? Of course, not! Would you wait half of an hour for a burger? Yeah! What approximately running a whole week for a brand-new TV? This is going into cost savings and will assist you, and your mind apprehends the cost of what you're buying and the possibility price of what you're shopping for.

7) Boom Profits Instead of Lessening Expenses

The remaining tip for shopping cash is a mentality

shift. In case you're saving money for the reason you want to buy something extravagant, the advice I'm able to come up with is to focus extra on how you may grow your earnings instead. Focusing on how you may make extra money will assist dramatically more than focusing on reducing your fees. Lower back to that balance statement, beefing up that earnings spot with the aid of $300 a month can be way less difficult than reducing my phone, insurance, gasoline, and a couple of other entertainment objects. I guess you've got a couple of hours on your life to spend operating a chunk greater, if now not on the organization you're employed at, working for your lifestyles through starting an enterprise or making an investment on your mind with the aid of analyzing.

Eight Mental Study Hints – A way to have a look at more fabric and analyze quicker

Have you ever pulled an all-nighter for a look at? Or long past into your room to study and simply felt misplaced on some of the questions? There are times wherein we simply do not study or analyze correctly, and we need to improve on that. It feels satisfying to instinctively know the solution to questions and even better to get a high grade in a tough course. I went through most of my high paying career simply soaking up the facts without having to look at in any respect, but now that I'm in university, I should prepare and, in reality, work on my own time to earn my grades. Today, we'll be going over eight psychological examine tips to help you look at greater and examine faster.

Tip #1: Use Specific Media

Like lot of you, I watch my animated motion pictures on eBook evaluations instead of simply reading the eBook, you have to be the use of special methods of analyzing. You may not have any motivation to study the eBook, have slower analyzing competencies, and watching a video with equal information will help you immensely more. Have a look at in 2008 states that "The greater regions of the brain that store facts about a subject, the more interconnection there's, this redundancy method students could have greater possibilities to drag up all of these associated bits of statistics from their multiple storage areas in reaction to a single cue."

There are numerous ways that you could use this key. One very well-known website is Khan Academy, in which you can watch films, entire exercise questions as well as ask people within the community about troubles that you've had. Some different examples of switching your look at strategies are flashcards, YouTube videos, audio sports, and apps consisting of Quizlet as well as just studying with buddies at a library or over Skype.

Tip #2: Spread Studying Through The Years

Many students cram at the entire day and if you're looking this video at the same time as cramming, then you can, however, use this, just less correctly than if you had planned higher. Making plans is a key aspect of existence and can be carried out right here. If you have a look at Friday and it is currently Monday, then spread the reading over the ones five days. You may have lots much less pressure, a lot less work each day, and will virtually recall it higher due to the fact every day you are best working on a sure sector of the chapter, leaving greater room for cognizance.

However, it might appear counter-intuitive for the majority, you'll be higher off observe a chapter an afternoon instead of 5 Chapters unexpectedly. Be self-conscious, though. You can be inside the small class in which this doesn't work, and you simply should realize the way you examine kindness. The identical idea applies to essays. In preference to writing it all in sooner or later and staying up till 3:00 a.m., every day of the week, write one paragraph, and in preference to three hours in the future, you get it completed with half-hour a day and a higher grade.

Tip #3: Connect What You're Leaning With Something You Understand

That is a key tip. On every occasion I had associated a concept in magnificence to something outdoor of college, I would take into account it because I knew it honestly implemented to my lifestyles, instead of being something trivial that wouldn't amount to whatever in real life. For example, in biology, we have been studying that energy could in no way be created or destroyed; however, it will be transferred or modified from one form to another. I had simply completed analyzing a book on how any impediment maybe was an advantage, so terrible power became an excellent factor genuinely due to the fact you certainly have something that you can convert into fantastic electricity, so the equal idea held here in which you may smash Dark energy.

However, you could use it for something effective. An instance is in case you are irritated, it's proper you've got the power. Many thoughts in technological know-how, records, English, and Math practice in actual life conditions. Think about how history repeats itself or how you could use the English language to speak more correctly as a frontrunner, or maybe in case you own a commercial enterprise, how you must be correct with numbers to be successful. Another thrilling, but beneficial instance is to use any shape of connection feasible. For example, my brother was studying for his states and capital assessments in 5th grade. I taught him that Florida looked like a proper, a tallywacker. I then informed him what tallywacker intended and he related the tallywacker concept to Tallahassee, and to these days, however, he recalls what the capital is. It doesn't rely upon if it's politically wrong or crude or something if it works, it works, and that's what will get you a terrific grade at the check. Just don't write tallywacker as the capital for Florida.

Tip #4: Test Yourself

This is self-explanatory. If you quiz yourself and you do nicely, the self-reassurance will lead to a better grade and will show you where you want to improve. There are numerous approaches to try this, one in every of that is searching up practice exams online, looking at questions in textbooks, in addition to quizzing yourself with pals. There's no excuse not to try this as there are so many sources on the internet. The usage of this, you may see what you're efficient at and gained waste time studying the things you recognize. Once more, Quizlet is a first-rate web page to go to for this in a pinch. Additionally, typing within the preliminary questions and solutions will substantially help.

Tip #5: Get Sleep

I get it, in case you're cramming now or have pulled all-nighters in the past, then it can repay now and again. On the other hand, as a popular rule of thumb, you want to be getting at least 7 hours of sleep a night to function properly. In case you're no longer getting enough sleep, your IQ simply drops if examined as you are not capable of think as fast, and your mental IQ drops. This will snowball into extra pressure, lower grades, or even less sleep inside the future. If you sleep four hours a night every night, you will burn out. Now, it is not the most effective result of being depressing. That's unfortunate in this situation, but additionally to gaining fats and turning into much less and less energetic. There are rumors Einstein slept 10 hours an afternoon and had daytime naps as properly, showing that even a genius needs to sleep.

Tip #6: Take A Seat At The Front

People who sit at the front of classes almost always get higher grades than the ones in the back. In a few training in which you are seated alphabetically, you could ask to take a seat in the front due to the fact "You may see clearer." It may be the stereotype that the more serious students take a seat inside the returned or simply the truth that it's more difficult to pay attention while you're no longer being watched by the instructor, however, in this case you need to apply the facts to gain an advantage for yourself, pick out a seat in the front. If this isn't possible for a few reasons (which may be very hardly ever the case), then pay attention closer in detail. That is more important than studying many topics because the teacher is the one who makes the exams and will give pointers inadvertently or purposefully, helping you recognize what is critical to know for the check and what is not. Asking the teacher questions during classes can even boost the information you retain while studying.

Tip #7: Use Have A Look At Breaks

For me, analyzing gets unproductive if I try to focus for too long of time; that's why cramming is ineffective after a while. You must take breaks. What I love to do is smash my work into chunks. As an instance, if I must examine 20 pages of a textbook one night, then I'm able to split that into chunks of five pages each, studying intensely, after which take a 5-minute spoil in among each chunk. This lets in me to flourish in the method and not see it as a frightening undertaking of reading 20 pages in one sitting unless the analyzing captures my interest and I will put it down. It's been verified that when at the 45-minute mark your retention will begin to decline. However, after a five-minute break for walking, stretching, or watching an enjoyable YouTube video, you will have enough strength for another 45 minutes of analyzing. In any case you want an extra clinical approach to this method, test out the Pomodoro approach.

Tip #8: Exercising

That is more of a life-style tip, but your whole lifestyle is more crucial after one look at it. Much like drowsing, workout gives you the energy to enjoy lifestyles. I would substitute life experience and work out well for the most part, likely messing up on one check-in place of cramming for a take a look at, feeling drained for the following couple of days, and now not having bad habits. Taking care of your physical health makes you feel better about yourself. I'm no longer pronouncing that bad humans are horrific humans, but in case you want to do well in courting, social conditions, and have greater self-assurance, then having a healthy body will help dramatically.

CHAPTER 4

DARK PSYCHOLOGY & MANIPULATION IN RELATIONSHIPS

The Devil's Desire

Seduction and sexual conquests are such common reasons and features of Dark psychology that they deserve their own individual chapter. Almost all and sundry have a chum who has been seduced by someone using deceit and manipulation. Perhaps in your own personal relationships, you have tried to use a few forms of underhanded manipulation to turn things into your favor.

The human urge to have intercourse is one of the most powerful urges and an inability to fulfill it could result in notable strain, fear, and disappointment in someone's lifestyles. Conversely, several the maximum famous historical figures are regarded for their numerous and successful conquests. Kings and emperors have regularly been afforded the most beautiful women within their world as a reward for his or her social standing.

One well known example of a powerful seducer is King Henry, the 8ᵗʰ of Britain. His urge for food and for girls was so robust that he created a new spiritual motion with a purpose to permit him to marry as many girls as he wished. Additionally, he took complete control over his many conquest's lives, several of them ending up beheaded at his own command.

However, King Henry, the 8ᵗʰ is one historical instance of the position of seduction and desire in the international of Dark psychology. The superiority of this topic and motivation are a sign that bureaucracy is a key aspect of Dark psychology. A failure to recognize how seduction and desire relate to Dark psychology leaves a student with incomplete knowledge of the subject.

Is all seduction Dark mental seduction? No. All seduction entails the pursuit of every other man or woman. Most of the people who aren't adept at the skills of Dark psychological manipulators, do that in a completely clumsy and unstructured way. To demonstrate this concept, consider the traditional romantic comedy setup with an inept man making a mistake after mistake in his pursuit of the female. A skilled psychological seducer is more like Ryan Gosling in Crazy, Stupid Love, or Will Smith in Hitch. They understand what they need and recognize the way to get it.

As you may see in this chapter, the usage of Dark psychology in the pursuit of seduction is neither inherently excellent nor is it awful. This can best be judged when it comes to the effect it has on the individual seduced. An entire segment of this chapter is devoted to know-how the difference in outcome among moral and immoral seduction.

How can this chapter be used? Within the basic understanding of it, it'll change whole your understanding of Dark psychology as a standard concept. Now, any book not containing element on seduction could be an incomplete work. Additionally, you could make real use of the information you choose whether you pick out to defend yourself and your loved ones from Dark seducers or come to be one yourself, is your choice.

This chapter will change the way you notice the dating world all the time.

Why Dark Psychological Seduction?

One of the essential questions human beings frequently have when they come across the concept of Dark psychological seduction for the primary time is "Why?" Why do humans select this precise path of attraction? Is it now not better to move on dates and court someone slowly and in reality? Knowledge, why human beings pick out the route of Dark seduction, is the first step in understanding their monstrous influence.

Permits don't forget someone who goes approximately their love life without using any ideas or strategies located within the global of dark psychology. This individual could be called a "Conventional Dater." This traditional dater spends loads of money and time on someone before they ever obtain experience with them sexually. They will marry them and make a public promise of faithfulness and commitment regardless of what.

Later down the road, the conventional dater, now the conventional spouse may additionally deduce that their life isn't as they imagined. They and their partner rushed into the wedding and it has no longer filled the expectations that they had for it. Each companion is left with a desire to either stay in a dull and unsatisfactory marriage or cheat on their partner. Who would want either path?

This sad conventional statistic can be contrasted with the carefree seducer who uses Dark psychology to get anything they want out of the place of romance. No other character is just too crucial to them because they understand their use of Dark psychology means they'll constantly be capable of discovering someone else. This makes them method lifestyles with a carefree, non-needy attitude.

If a carefree seducer does select to relax finally, they do so with none feeling of "Settling" or rushing into the first dating they have got haphazardly stumbled throughout. This ends in a happier, content marriage as it's miles from an area of abundance in place of scarcity.

How can a carefree seducer have a lot of fulfillment and influence inside the relationship world? It's due to the strength of the concepts they apprehend and the skill they've in executing the techniques that stem from the ideas. For the duration of this eBook, you have seen limitless examples of ways Dark psychology can work in several of regions of existence. Why would the arena of courting and seduction be one-of-a-kind?

One of the key blessings that users of Dark psychology have over their competition is that their expertise in the human mind is almost like a secret weapon. If conventional statistics is a clumsy man stumbling blindly by the world of romance, accepting something takes place to come back his way, the skilled seducer is a sniper, searching, and playing something, they show up to crave on time.

A person who tries out the ideas of Dark psychology inside the courting international is possibly to be amazed at how their reports differ from their past efforts. A sense of control and self-assurance replaces a beyond one of doubt, neediness, and lack of confidence. Amazingly, the Dark psychology consumer will no longer most effectively find that they sense higher about their effects. Additionally, they may see that the human beings they're interacting with are taking part in enjoying plenty greater as nicely. This is because Dark psychology teaches a seducer exactly what people are seeking out within the romantic world, in addition, it teaches the seducer how to provide it to them seamlessly.

Many people who have applied their mental knowledge to the sector of relationship and seduction for the first time describe it as a surprising moment. The use of these strategies and ideas offers them the capacity to, in the end, get what they need from lifestyles and satisfy their innermost, longest-held desires.

Is Dark Seduction Evil?

One of the most common queries inexperienced individuals flock to is the idea of Dark psychological seduction, is whether the strategies are immoral or evil in some way. Like almost something, Dark mental seduction is neither inherently top nor bad. The way it is used determines the quantity to which it can be judged morally. Plainly speaking, human beings use Dark psychological seduction involving one of three possible motivations—to help the people they seduce, to hurt the people they seduce, or to best help themselves.

Many human beings find it difficult to trust that anyone could pass into the world of Dark mental seduction with the reasoning of helping the other person. Truly, all seducers are selfish and careless, right? Wrong.

One of the most famous thoughts from the world of seduction is "Go away them higher than you discovered them." Individuals who keep this viewpoint, experience that there's no need for someone to "Lose" inside the process of seduction. Both parties, the seducer and the character being seduced, can enjoy a "Win/Win" experience where no one loses out.

How does someone experience a seductive lifestyle while making sure they leave people higher than they found them? By no means, lying or deceptive, a victim outright is a key idea in the back of ethical seduction. One of the most common hallmarks of insincere human beings is "Leading on" by promising the world and in return not receiving anything. Experienced seducers do now not make guarantees they cannot live up to. Instead, they genuinely allow the character they may be seducing to get caught up within the moment and enjoy it absolutely.

Other people enter the world of Dark psychological

destruction with less devious motives. They only want fulfill their hopes and dreams, and they will gladly mislead, harm, or harm the individual they're seducing. Such uncaring narcissism is ironically appealing to a few people who, bizarrely, and go back the familiar behavior of being used time and time again.

The behavior of someone who is going about their mental seduction without a care other than their delight frequently ends up causing them problems. If humans pass into the arena of seduction without a very carefree, nihilistic mindset, problems can stand up. Regularly, this form of seducer finally ends up in a scenario of having unwanted kids and having to pay several child support payments. In addition, they may be more likely to invoke the fury of scorned conquests, they have carelessly discarded. Those who are too cavalier of their seductive efforts have even been murdered through jealous or hurt former fanatics.

Main processes to Dark psychological seduction have now been explored folks that intend to help others and people whose goal to harm others. We can now look at the 1/3 method—the individual that thinks best in their very own enjoy.

Such people, as just described, are more likely to derive amusement from their exploration and manipulation of social regulations and conventions as they are from the romance they control to reap. Of course, this form is like the only walked by a person who goes from overweight to healthful through a centered collection of effort and self-betterment. The impact they have got upon the people they are seducing is much less important to them than the impact their Dark seduction has on themselves.

The Place to Begin of Seduction

You now understand the basic idea of Dark psychological seduction and the reasons people choose to use it. You also are conscious that such people may be appropriate, awful, or detached. Now the motive and intention of mental seducers are clean, how exactly do they do what they do?

Most seducers are likely to have a "Guiding Method" that undermines their efforts in addition to precise processes that stem from this philosophy. In our exploration of this, one of the kind philosophies, we can see many familiar ideas from dark psychology. Seduction is often the place in which thoughts are moved from an abstract idea into applied practice.

One technique to Dark mental seduction is the deployment of a biased, inflexible method. Such seducers sense that they've mapped out the collection of attraction to a near flowchart like the level of precision and element. They see the technique of psychological seduction as predictable and replicable. Their systems are possible to work for them, however, also others in general who're capable of understanding and enforce them properly.

A trademark of such seducers is their utilization of a sequence of various tiers. A few will try to lead their goal via a dependent range of emotions—consisting of the hobby, accompanied by way of appeal accompanied by the aid of pleasure. Such seducers see their seduction method as a chain of checkpoints to skip via to gain their eventual aim.

One of the strengths of an established gadget of seduction is folks that observe a feeling of truth that they always realize what to do next. They mustn't fear what to do subsequent because the technique is as routine and ordinary as driving a vehicle or brushing teeth. A disadvantage to this inflexible method is that it can cause problems whilst a person isn't always responding as meant. Now, structured seducers and then lose sight of the fact that people are an unpredictable as opposed to a predictable computer program.

The approach to seduction that is the strongest in comparison to the dependent technique is the "Herbal" method. This includes cultivating authentic emotional states similar to the seducer and then freely expressing them to the person they want to seduce. For instance, a person using this type of unstructured seduction is likely to spend time on their emotional make-up and outlook and how to best it. In addition, they express this externally to different humans.

NLP (Neuro-Linguistic Programming) and hypnotic seduction is a subset of dark mental seduction and the thoughts that undermine the general concept. Not like based seduction or the greater natural version, NLP/hypnotic seduction involves triggering emotional states in the person who is the target of seduction after which linking these states to the hypnotic seducer.

As an example, the NLP technique to seduction may involve permitting a person to discover their excessive feelings, after which "Anchoring" the cause for those feelings to the person that brought about them, the seducer. The seducer is then able to cause intense pride of their sufferer through issuing the anchor, inclusive of a gesture, tone or words.

Hypnotic seduction is a hard approach to use often. That is because few things placed a person's shield up as plenty as the marginally bizarre strategies worried in NLP. Structured or unstructured seduction at the least comes throughout as "Ordinary," whereas hypnotic seduction does not. Some people respond thoroughly to it, however, and people who do are possibly to be better in shape in personal compatibility with the hypnotic seducer.

Some psychological seducers are capable of invert conventional seduction dynamics and gender roles to high-quality impact. For example, the standard view of seduction, at some point in history, is that the man is aggressive, and the lady plays a passive role. Inverting these roles may lead to powerful outcomes. Some guys find that they're able to allow themselves to become the prize, the one who's chased. This inversion of the social norm can cause a refreshing exchange from the mundane habits of courting for anyone concerned.

Girl mental seducers are also able to use the inversion of traditional seduction dynamics to powerful effect. A few men are crushed if the lady is the aggressive, confident pursuer, and a whole lot of ladies additionally recall feeling a sense of empowerment and proactivity that they have got no longer skilled inside their romantic life at any time before.

Some humans also input the world of psychological seduction intending to break loose from the constraints of monogamy that have held them back during their lifestyles. This technique is now and again known as polyamory, an open dating, or a few different versions on this subject matter depending on the want of the individual pursuing it. By using gaining knowledge of Dark psychological techniques, this type of seducer can pursue their real dreams in a way this is open, honest, and effective.

The Techniques

You now understand the "Guiding Ideas" behind mental processes to seduction and the motivations that people have for sporting them out. How exactly do people move approximately translating those thoughts and theories into actionable ideas and strategies?

The "Indirect Approach" is a key technique within the international of seduction. One mistake that many people make within the international of conventional dating is presenting a tacky and unappealing icebreaker while introducing themselves to an ability seduction goal.

"Nice Eyes," "You look good," And "Great song, right?" Some of these are examples of some of the most clichéd icebreakers out there. Why are those so terrible? Women are possible to have heard them countless times before and are instantly turned off upon listening to them. While a seducer uses such a lousy line, it suggests they are a bland and unappealing character.

The refreshing opener is a breath of clean air in comparison to its clichéd precedents. An indirect opener is any icebreaking gambit that initiates a social interplay without conveying sexual reasons. That is regularly posed inside the shape of a "Fascinating Query," as an example, a seducer using an oblique opener would possibly ask, "Settle this for my friends or me over there—do guys or women lie more?" This sparks a conversation and suggests the seducer to be an exciting character who's searching out, not looking for anything other than a great conversation.

In addition, indirect openers have the advantage of doing away with the opportunity of rejection. A person, the use of an oblique opener, is not "Imparting" themselves in any manner to the character they desire to seduce, and it's thought not possible to "Reject" something or someone that has no longer been "Supplied."

Social proof is any other key method within the global of Dark mental seduction. Those who are popular are instantly more appealing than folks who are not. Why? It's human extinct to assume that if someone is widely appreciated, there may be something likable about them. All and sundry's worst nightmare is being seduced through some creepy loner without buddies and nobody they're near. A person like that is likely to be higher lonely and needy.

How can social proof be used in the place of psychological seduction? This is a case in which "Showing is more effective than telling." Many people make the mistake of bragging about their reputation or success in a way that comes across as bragging or a few different shapes of striving tough, unnatural conduct. It's far better to truly be at a booth in a club or bar with a group of interesting people. This conveys social value without rubbing it in a person's face.

One use of social evidence is, devious. Let's picture a psychological seducer in a bar or club environment. They see a woman; they need to move and speak to her. Rather than approaching the woman directly, they approach a nearby individual to strike up a conversation. Then move on with confidence to the person they had originally meant to talk to. They rather test this technique on another person first, strike up a conversation with them, move over to their original goal and start interacting with the originally meant character. This gets rid of the notion of loneliness that would otherwise exist. Furthermore, it could spark a little jealous contention among the two women!

Being something of a project is a Dark mental method outside of the draw close of maximum conventional daters. Most people make the mistake of being too eager and too to be had. An example might be a person who frivolously waits at the same time as a few women in a bar ignores him absolutely or a lady who places up with a few shapes of disloyal or disrespectful behavior from the man or woman they may be with. The alternative of this display of low private standards is a show of being "Hard to get." this may take several forms.

One approach that uses the "Challenging" precept is to stroll far from a seduction target if needed. As an instance, if the goal is being cheeky or sassy, the seducer can playfully say "You're nice," and turn to stroll away. In most instances, the goal may be wowed by this unconventional conduct and experience interacting with someone who has requirements and self-belief.

Every other way of being challenging is by way of the use of cautiously chosen and playfully teases all through the route of an interaction. Although the general public trying to seduce a person, are excessively fine. They provide compliments after praise, laugh at all the jokes they make, listen and usually do the whole lot to imprison their notion inside the confines of "Satisfactory but bland." With the aid of throwing out a playful tease, the seducer gives an amusing emotional "Spike" which sparks attraction within the character they wish to seduce.

One of the main motivations behind human revel in is to be seeking out, that's new and interesting. That is specifically authentic in the world of romance, wherein most of the people are searching out something amusing and exciting. There's a purpose that clichéd strains and dating profiles are these sorts of a regular punch line because they're dull and don't genuinely paintings. An antidote to the disease of blandness is getting to know the way to stand out amazingly.

The idea of standing out amazingly can be positioned into practice by using first considering what everybody else is doing wrong. Once that is clear, the seducer must keep in mind how these incorrect actions might make the seduction goal experience. Once that is understood, the seducer can put the pieces collectively to answer the question of "How am I able to do matters differently from absolutely everyone else in a way that might make the alternative person reply properly?"

Some of the maximum commonplace ways of status out in an amazing way consist of dressing a little better or a bit greater apparently than other human beings inside the venue. For instance, if an area could be very casual, dressing up simply can be very beneficial. Nobody is suggesting you wear a tuxedo to a sports bar but making a bit more of an attempt can be very powerful indeed.

Organizing a frame of main is every other useful approach inside the global of psychological seduction. Most of the people are glad to be led. Indecisiveness is one of the least appealing features in an individual. Approaches of showing decisiveness and the capability to steer include bodily transferring around a venue, suggesting an exchange of venue, and not being afraid to disagree with something that is stated. Many humans, men make the mistake of behaving contrary to this principle by being an indecisive leaf in the wind as opposed to a strong, assured alpha male who is aware of that they need in life.

A natural extension of knowing a way to lead knows a way to close. Spend a while speaking to the girls on your life and they're likely to proportion many personal experiences of guys who had been wishy-washy and indecisive when it turned into a time for the first kiss, first sexual stumble upon, or some other romantic milestone. Hesitation at the part of a lady also can be off setting for guys. Think about it. Who wants to be with someone who doesn't even realize what they need? Decisiveness and the ability to act are key components in making sure a mental seduction is going as intended.

Some mental seducers are able to harness Dark mental tendencies, which include factors of psychopathy in pursuit of their romantic pursuits. One of the trademark features of a psychopath is a capacity to now not sense fear while interacting with other humans. Most men and women are paralyzed with the aid of worry, especially the fear of rejection from a person they're romantically inquisitive about. A selected approach exists that may be learned from the instance of fearless psychopaths and used to conquer this fear.

How exactly does a person conquer their worry of

rejection? Simple. With the aid of being rejected time and time again and figuring out, it is not sure that horrific. Over the years, mental seducers examine that it is usually higher to be the individual that attempted and failed than the individual that didn't have the self-belief to attempt. Taking motion becomes its praise and the seducer loses their anxiety and hesitation inside the procedure.

Those who positioned this desensitization to rejection method into motion will begin to recognize that the less they fear rejection, the much less it takes place. Being assured and calm while interacting with new human beings is one of the byproducts of this approach. The more someone gets rejected, to begin with, the less they will fear future rejections. This translates into actual achievement and much less rejection in the end! Attempt it and see.

CHAPTER 5
DARK PSYCHOLOGY &
MANIPULATION IN WORKSPACES

What Does Mental Manipulation Contain?

Manipulation in the business global and paintings cultures often depends upon hidden agendas. It also includes an attempt to coerce or subtly manipulate any other man or woman into giving in or doing what the manipulator desires them to suppose, experience, or do.

Psychological manipulation is in which a person uses underhand, deceptive techniques, disguising aggression as accurate intentions, and who's a professional at maintaining their motives beneath wraps. Right here are a few of the most common symptoms of a manipulator at work:

- Superficial appeal and false sympathy

- Negotiations that don't sense truthful, with no win-win solutions

- Verbal intimidation or insincere reward

- Meetings where you unexpectedly leave loaded down with work – with an unfair quantity of monkeys in your lower back

- Passive-competitive behavior

- Human beings kept in the dark about critical selections, with critical information withheld

- The weather of distrust in which there may be a perceived want to tread on eggshells

- Gossiping, putting humans in opposition to one another, spreading rumors

- Less clarity, extra developing confusion

- Bad morale growing at paintings

- Refusal to admit wrongdoing, tries to rationalize, making excuses, and acting surprised whilst confronted

The Way To Understand A Manipulator

A manipulator might also flatter you because you are the leader and initially appear very supportive of all you do. If they can nurture your acceptance as the ultimate truth, you may properly need you to treat them as a listening ear or a depended on a marketing consultant. If this happens, then you have played right into their fingers. Being on top of things of shaping how you see things might be exceedingly critical to them. Withholding records or spreading snippets of news, primarily based on some 'truths,' however, which create incorrect impressions. In their arms, statistics may be a weapon. Little lies, or 'almost' lies, can be part of their conversations.

Manipulators deliver off mixed messages to the ones around them. They use selective attention, giving it to others whilst it serves their purposes, but regularly absent or giving little attention in different circumstances. For their colleagues, this will be confusing and irritating.

Skilled manipulators don't want to fight their own battles or do their very dirty deeds. They'll search for someone else to do it for them, making sure they're not in the front line. Manipulators will work difficult at positioning themselves advantageously in organizations.

They will rarely take responsibility for their

movements or preserve themselves accountable inside the equal manner others do. Additionally, they've 'Teflon' traits. They may be exceptional victims, producing guilt, support, care, and masses of interest. In this way, they make others feel obligated to help them or finish projects that they should be doing themselves. They can evoke the need to be rescued.

Generally, there are adept at sowing the seeds of guilt and confusion, making people feel they're somehow in the wrong or must be doing more. Certainly, they take themselves very seriously and react to the whole thing extremely personal.

Why Do They Do It?

What do people gain from being manipulators? It's usually right down to getting what they want, something like an object or pay raise, and in the back of that lies a yearning for strength, a need to feel advanced, to constantly be right, to win no matter what it expenses. On the other hand, it isn't about electricity and it's without a doubt all approximately emotional weakness – an excellent issue to recall.

How Does Manipulation Affect The Place Of Job?

A manipulator can ship a talented workforce to the closest recruitment firm looking for a brand-new task. They pit people against a different situation, set their colleagues up for failure, and force already-strained running relationships over the threshold. Manipulators smash tasks and kill closing dates, alternate the emotional climate profoundly, make their colleagues depressed, and preserve people in a nation of a disappointment for as long as they want. They depend upon secrecy and on different human beings' correct will and reticence.

Do They Recognize They're Doing It?

Some do, some don't. Whether or not they're self-aware or no longer, a manipulator's behavior is regularly compulsive. They tend to journey themselves up over the years. After they reveal their hand and their behaviors are exposed, they may then determine to move on or need to be moved on. One manner or the alternative matters don't live the identical, it can be a manner of when they have left, there's a few emotional mopping up for all and sundry else to do.

How To Defuse A Manipulator?

As a leader, how do you address a manipulator? Your first step is to recognize that even as they could look like an effective hazard, most manipulators are very dependent upon others to reinforce their identity. After you and your personnel prevent being fearful, these vulnerable characters can lose the most of their power. With this attention, you may begin to benefit strength and begin to muster up the courage to act differently.

Your best strategy is to consciously realize what's happening and now not deny it. After you're privy to their approaches, you could push back. Pushing again regularly approach speaking to a person you trust. You will be surprised to discover you're now not the only one who feels that way. If the manipulator is skilled, you've probably been thinking you're going crazy. Identifying and talking to others within the manipulator's field of operation will make it clear, you are sane after all!

It's essential to preserve yourself steady and secure. Don't consider anything that the manipulator says and never supply them any private, work-related, or exclusive situations approximately close to yourself or your role.

This can be difficult when you consider that they're notoriously good at producing considerably unique situations that turn into their favor. Just consider any records you deliver them; they may sooner or later use against you.

It may be difficult while you're in work, but it enables you to minimize the interactions you've got together with your administrative center manipulator, minimizing the encounters you can't keep away from, quick and expert. If they stop through your desk to the percentage of different people's problems with you, hoping you'll join in, don't get concerned. Gossip is considered one of their biggest weapons, so don't interact with it. If you like, simply say, "I don't do gossip" and shrink back.

Taking A Robust Stand

As a leader, you might need to take a firm stance on your group's behalf because you're accountable for their nicely-being at work. Be honest with yourself. Let your 'sure' be 'yes,' and your 'no' be 'no.' In the beginning, the manipulator may come off even tougher; however, at heart, those humans are cowards. Don't respond to attempted guilt journeys. As a leader, this is the time while you need to hold your ground and act from your strong integral base.

If you have been studying this book and several the situations resonate with you, get in touch to explore how training can help you.

CHAPTER 6
DARK PSYCHOLOGY & MANIPULATION USED BY CHILDREN & DAD, AND MOM

Children of narcissists undergo a lifetime's worth of abuse. Narcissistic dad and mom lack empathy, take advantage of their children for their very own agendas and are not going to are seeking treatment or alternate their adverse behaviors for long-time (Kacel, Ennis, & Pereira, 2017). This shape of trauma places kids of narcissists at danger for suicide, low self-esteem, depression, self-harm, substance abuse, attachment disorders, and complex PTSD (Post-Traumatic Stress Disorder), leading to signs just like children who were mentally, emotionally, verbally or sexually abused (Gibson, 2016; Schwartz, 2016; Spinazzola et al., 2014; Walker, 2013).

If youngsters of narcissists choose to stay in contact with their abusive dad and mom, they will be on track to be susceptible of manipulation at the same time as adults. The identical techniques which have been employed to control them as kids can, however, be effective even if they are adults – perhaps even more, so because these techniques force them to regress lower back into early life states of worry, disgrace, and terror.

The distinction is that as a grownup, you can apply opportunity coping methods, self-care, and to restrict contact with your mother and father as you heal. Right here, there are five manipulation strategies narcissistic dad and mom use to manipulate their children, even as adults, and some self-care suggestions for coping:

1) Emotional Blackmail

The narcissistic discern to make a request, but it is truly a demand. If you say no, set barriers or let them realize you'll get back to them later, they'll observe improved strain and threaten consequences to try and get you to acquiesce to them. However, in case you refuse, they will then punish you with sulking, passive-aggressive statements, a rage attack, withholding of something essential, or even the hazard of violence or sabotage. This is emotional blackmail.

Example: Your narcissistic mom may tell you that she would like you and your own family to come back over at the weekend for dinner. All the family can be there and that they want to see you. Understanding her abusive methods, you inform her you cannot make it this weekend due to the fact you've got a prior engagement. As opposed to respecting your desires, she proceeds to speak about how ungrateful you're being and how all your family members are looking forward to seeing you and your kids. You are saying no and she or he hangs up on you and treats you to the silent treatment for weeks.

Self-Care Tip: know your rights and boundaries. You have got proper to say "No" to any invitation or request, specifically from a person recognized to be abusive. You've got the right to defend yourself and every other circle of relative's participants who might be affected by your toxic parent's conduct. You don't need to give into any silent treatments or tolerate rage attacks. You may allow your narcissistic parent to have anything response they've from a distance. All through this time, do not answer cellphone calls, textual content messages, or voicemails abusive in nature. Do not meet with them in character to "Speak." Your "No" is not a negotiation.

2) Guilt-Tripping With Fear, Obligation, & Guilt (FOG)

It's not unusual for narcissistic mother and father to apply FOG (Fear, Obligation, & Guilt) on us to awaken the kind of guilt that would reason us to give in to their dreams, even at the price of our very own needs and rights.

Example: Your narcissistic father disapproves of the truth that you're unmarried and have no children. He tells you that point is running out to provide him, grandchildren. When you tell him you're happy being unmarried, he lashes out in rage and melancholy, telling you, "So I'm going to die without grandchildren? I get older and sicker every day – don't you think I need to see my daughter begin a family? Is this the way you're repaying me for all I've completed for you? What's going to our network assume, to look a single woman at your age? It's shameful and disgraceful! You're a shame to the family!"

Self-Care Tip: Word any guilt or disgrace that arises

and realize it does no longer belong to you while you discover your self being guilt-tripped by a narcissistic discern. Ask yourself if you have something to feel guilty approximately. Have you ever deliberately inflicted any damage upon your narcissistic figure or are you doing what everyone has a right to do – live their lives on their own free will? You have a right for your choices, choices, and autonomy, even in case your poisonous discern disagrees with those choices. You no longer owe them an explanation for choices that must do with your profession, love lifestyles, or any kids you may or may not have.

3) Shaming

Narcissistic, toxic mother and father disgrace their youngsters to, besides, belittle and demean them. That is quite effective, as research has shown that once a person feels mistaken and defective, they tend to be more compliant to the requests of others (Walster, 1965; Gudjonsson and Sigurdsson, 2003).

Instance: Your narcissistic figure starts commenting upon your career choices all through Thanksgiving dinner, calling them reckless, and irresponsible. Although you are a hit, financially stable, and own your home, they keep nitpicking at approaches you fall short of because you didn't pick the career they'd demanded of you. They criticize your capability to provide on your own family and to be a position model for your children.

Self-Care Tip: Well known in case you're having any shape of emotional flashback while your figure begins to nitpick and disgrace you. It's essential to notice in case you sense you're regressing lower back to adolescence states of powerlessness so that you can learn to take your energy again inside the present moment instead of reacting in a manner that offers into their shaming procedures. Let them recognize you can't be shamed and that if they retain this conduct, they'll simply see less of you. Apprehend that this shame does no longer belong to you and remind yourself of how some distance you've come. You deserve to be pleased with yourself, not ashamed.

4) Triangulation and Comparison

Narcissistic mother and father love to examine their kids to different siblings or peers if you want to similarly lessen them. They need their scapegoated youngsters to fight for their approval and interest. Additionally, they want to initiate them into feeling less than.

Instance: You get a call from your parents who tell you the information about your cousin getting engaged. Your toxic mom makes a snide comment like, "You know, your cousin Ashley just completed medical school and got engaged. What are you doing with your life?"

Self-Care Tip: Don't give into petty comparisons – label them as triangulation and recognize it is just some other manner to undermine you. Change the issue or discover an excuse to cut the verbal exchange short in case your narcissistic figure engages in unnecessary comparisons and disparaging comments. Note if you have an urge to justify or explain yourself –resist the urge to accomplish that.

Recognize that you no longer need to waste your energy, proving your accomplishments to folks who are unwilling to know them. Spend time with those who do celebrate you and keep a list of what you're proud of to remind yourself, which you do not should evaluate yourself to all of us with a purpose to sense a success to your personal proper.

5) Gaslighting

Gaslighting is an insidious weapon in the toolbox of a narcissistic figure. It lets in the toxic discern to distort reality, deny the truth of the abuse, and make you feel like the toxic one for calling them out.

Example: Your narcissistic father leaves you an abusive voicemail overdue at nighttime and ten neglected calls while you refuse to change your mind to do something for him. Even though you've explained to him that it's inconvenient for you to do, he persists in punishing you for now, not complying with his requests and continues to badger you through the phone. The following day, you name him to confront him about his harassing conduct, and he responds by saying, "You're making a mountain out of a molehill. I was barely talked to you last night. You're imagining things."

Self-Care Tip: People who are gaslighted in formative years regularly suffer from a chronic feeling of self-doubt in maturity. In place of giving into your conditioned experience of self-doubt, start to word every time your narcissist figure's falsehoods no longer measure up with the truth. While you experience an abusive incident, report it and work with a therapist to stay grounded in what you've skilled in each childhood and adulthood in preference to subscribing to the toxic parent's version of occasions.

Track if there's been a pattern of gaslighting in your dating along with your narcissistic determine and act as a result with what you've lived through, in place of what the abusive discern claims. Don't forget, the more you resist abuse amnesia, the more likely you'll be able to shield yourself and avoid being exploited or taken benefit of through the poisonous experiences.

CHAPTER 7
SIGNS WHICH YOU ARE BEING MANIPULATED

Flattery is a manipulator's favorite weapon. If you are one of these types of individuals, how can you refuse to help a terrible man in need? Be alert if any person starts off to mention good things about you completely out of nowhere.

1. Manipulators seek advice from someone else's advantageous revel in.

Some other preferred pass of every manipulator is the word "Don't fear, I (my buddy, my boss, a man I know) have completed this normally, and nothing terrible happened." It doesn't need to be counted that the manipulator's concept scares you. The most important issue is its fulfillment. Of course, it's a lie! Don't concentrate on such phrases. Ask for concrete proof.

2. Manipulators continually start communication at the worst time.

Manipulators love asking for assistance while you are very busy. This offers them a better chance that you will agree simply to get rid of them. They'll express regret and they may let you know how sorry they're to ask you for help at this second. Stay alert!

3. Manipulators remind you constantly about your guarantees.

"You promised me" is a high-quality word, so one can make you do something a manipulator tells you, even if you recognize something isn't right about it. No one wants to be the person that doesn't keep their word. No one wants to appear in this manner. Your answer must constantly be very clear so that nobody can blackmail you later.

4. Passive manipulators fake acting helpless and ditsy. They continually play the offended reasoning card.

You certainly want to help someone who appears to be an innocent and harmless lady. She is usually unfortunate and unhappy, and you need to hug her and deliver her shelter. This is precisely what she desires. Such "Sufferers" can even act like this unconsciously;

however, it doesn't make it much less of a manipulation.

5. Manipulators force you too hurried or quick emotional decisions.

All desirable manipulators recognize that fast emotional selections are their bread and butter. If they don't give you enough time to think about something or if they force you to make a fast decision, they win. An easy phrase like "I need time," if stated expectantly, will maximum likely cool the manipulator's eagerness, and she or he won't ask you once more.

6. Manipulators need you to experience guilt.

It is so easy to control someone who feels responsible. They are ready to help with anything. Be cautious in case you begin feeling guilty in the direction of anyone. Their small "Favors" are most likely coming.

7. You feel a sense of worry, duty, and guilt.

Manipulative behavior includes three elements, consistent with Stines: Fear, obligation, and guilt. You would possibly be scared to do it, obligated to do it, or guilty approximately no longer doing it.

She factors to 2 commonplace manipulators: "The

bully" and "The sufferer." A bully makes you sense fear and can use aggression, threats, and intimidation to control you, she says. The victim engenders a sense of guilt for their target. "The victim normally acts hurt," Stine says. However, at the same time, as manipulators frequently play the victim, the fact is that they may be the ones who've triggered the problem, she adds.

A person who's centered by way of manipulators who play the victim regularly try and help the manipulator to stop feeling responsible, Stines says. Targets of this sort of manipulation often experience accountable for assisting the sufferer by doing something they can stall their suffering.

8. You're wondering yourself.

The term "Gaslighting" is frequently used to discover manipulation that receives human beings to question themselves, their reality, reminiscence, or thoughts. A manipulative individual might twist what you and turn it back on you, hijack the verbal exchange, or make you feel such as you've finished something incorrectly while you're not quite certain you have, in step with Stines.

If you're being gaslighted, you may feel a fake experience of guilt or defensiveness, such as you failed or need to have accomplished something incorrect while that's not the case, in step with Stines.

"Manipulators blame," she says. "They don't take responsibility."

9. There are strings connected.

"If favor isn't executed for you simply due to the fact, then it isn't "For amusing and without spending a dime," says Stines.

Stines refers to 1 type of manipulator as 'Mr. Pleasant man.' This person is probably useful and does quite a few favors for different people.

Exploiting the norms and expectancies of reciprocity is one of the maximum common kinds of manipulation, says Jay Olson, a doctoral researcher studying manipulation at McGill college.

A shop clerk, as an instance, may make it appear like the fact he or she gave you a deal, you should buy the product. In a courting, an associate would possibly buy you flora then request something in go back.

10. You notice the 'foot-in-the-door' and 'door-in-the-face' techniques.

Regularly, manipulators try considered one of two strategies, says Olson. The primary is the foot-in-the-door method, in which someone starts with a small and affordable request like, do you have the time? Which then leads into a larger request like I want $10 for a taxi. The door-in-the-face technique is the opposite. It includes a person creating a huge request, having it rejected, then making a smaller one, Olson explains.

Someone doing settlement paintings, for instance, might also ask you for a massive sum of money upfront, and then once you decline, will ask for a smaller amount, he says.

17 Warning Symptoms of a Manipulator

Everyone people has come into touch with manipulators. Some people have been abused for years without them getting to know. Spotting a manipulator is tough because they work at stealth frequencies. It's a crime that leaves no fingerprints; however, there isn't always any sort of human conduct that you cannot recognize or predict.

Here are some early caution signs and symptoms with a purpose to warn you to a manipulator in your lifestyles:

- Allure and Niceness

- Denial

- Mendacity

- Beneficial with Favors and presents

- Excessive Compliments and Flattery

- Forced Teaming

- Correct First impression

- Pretending to be a sufferer

- Silent treatment

- Acting to be Selfless

- Guilt Tripping

- Shaming

- Intimidation

- Gasoline lighting fixtures

- Rationalization

- Diversion

- Unsettling Stare

1. Appeal and Niceness

A manipulator might also use attraction to get power or intercourse. The appeal comes without difficulty to manipulators because they're ruthless and have no qualms about hurting absolutely everyone. A reasonably conscientious person might not use the grimy hints to seduce someone that a manipulator will eagerly do.

Manipulators are ardent college students of human behavior. After spending a while with someone, they find out about their desires and goals. After they discover what you need, they offer you with it to get you addicted or dependent on them. If someone is very captivating and alluring to you, think about what that individual may want to possibly want. Manipulators use charm to seduce and mislead.

2. Denial

Manipulators are professionals at mendacity and

denying. If someone hurts you and you deliver attention to their bad behavior, but they deny it although they have behaved badly, you then should be on the defensive. Don't allow their denial of awful behavior to confuse you.

Psychologist, George K. Simon, a manipulation expert, and creator of the eBook in Sheep's apparel elucidate, ''This 'who…. Me?' tactic is a manner of gambling harmless and invites the sufferer to feel unjustified in confronting the aggressor approximately the inappropriateness of their conduct. Additionally it is the manner the aggressor offers himself/herself permission to maintain right on doing what they need to do.''

3. Mendacity

Mendacity is a manipulator's maximum potent weapon. They have got an impaired sense of right and wrong, so they don't sense horrific about lying. If there's a danger to get what they need by way of mendacity, they most likely will.

Manipulators typically lie in subtle, covert ways. Dr. Simon says that manipulators often lie by way of withholding a sizeable amount of statistics from you or with the aid of distorting the truth.

Correctly catching a liar can be discovered. To locate early on, whether you're managing a manipulator or no longer, ask them direct questions about his or her employment, the circle of relatives, spouse, children, friends, location of residence, plans, and so forth. If they supply vague, inconsistent, or evasive replies to you, this needs to function a red flag.

4. Generous with Favors and Items

Inside the starting of dating, a manipulator may be very kind, sympathetic, and generous towards you. He may also shower you with expensive items and favors, which you might interpret as an expression of his love or affection. On the other hand, without a doubt, he's using them as a form of bribery to get even larger favors later.

While a person showers you with gifts and attention, pay vital attention to the individual and aim of that man or woman.

5. Immoderate Compliments and Flattery

Psychologists Robert D. Hare and Paul Babaik in their

book Snakes in fits propose that ''Excessive or incongruous compliments need to be a signal so that it will pay vital attention to what's coming subsequent. Ask yourself, "What does this man or woman want of me?"

6. Forced Teaming

The manipulator tries to mission a shared motive or enjoys with you, where none exists. How do you tell if someone is honestly trying to be helpful or they may be just manipulating you? Listen to your instinct. Do you feel uncomfortable about accepting help? Do you need to refuse, but you may due to the fact this could make you appear rude? If sure, you then are managing a manipulator.

Ladies must not receive any provide of help that makes the experience uncomfortable.

7. True First Impact

Skilled manipulators often make the best first impressions. They use fascinating characteristics like impeccable manners, stunning seems, or a prevailing smile, etc., to distract human beings from their real intentions and message. We hardly purchase an eBook after being impressed through its cowl, but lamentably, we take people at face value. With manipulators, you don't get what you see.

A manipulator may additionally provide you with an excellent first impression; however, the cracks in their mask turn into obvious simplest after close observation or spending extra time with them.

8. Pretending to be a sufferer

A manipulator might also pretend as being a sufferer of occasions or horrific conduct of a person, as a result, making you sense sympathy for her or him.

When someone attempts to seek your sympathies, carefully examine at that person to attempt to affirm that they're indeed a sufferer.

How to inform a false victim from a real one?

A false sufferer talks about the events that had been abusive to them in a calm, cool, and detached way. They seem to get over the emotions of the abusive revel in as a substitute quickly. They don't seem to dwell or obsess over the abusive stories.

True victims need to reach out for aid; it's critical for

his or her survival. They seek remedy, God, or different saving techniques to repair their mental and emotional health. At the same time, as speaking about the abusive experience, they appear pressured, jumpy, anxious, and afraid. They'll cry hysterically—urgency and emotion are in their speech. They do now not have the cold, cool demeanor of a lying manipulator. Genuine sufferers go through the grieving process—shock, denial, and anger to finally the degree of recognition.

On the other hand, manipulators pretending to be victims don't try to are seeking that sort of assist. They don't need it due to the fact they have been now not abused. Manipulators pretending to be sufferers aren't in search of kindness and compassion; however, they're after an aim, so coolly and in control, they let you know their tale.

9. Silent Remedy

Getting "Silent Remedy" is an early warning signal that you are handling a manipulator. Manipulators use the silent treatment as a weapon to initiate you into doing something or make you feel much less worth through refusing to acknowledge even your presence. If an act of your behavior isn't always contributing towards the manipulator's purpose, they'll use silent remedy as a punishment to communicate their displeasure. This is the major reason why scientific psychologist experts, Harriet Braiker describe it as a form of manipulative punishment.

If it's a sadistic manipulator, then they may use silent treatment simply to torture you.

10. Acting To Be Selfless

Manipulators keep their intentions, ambitions, choice for energy and domination properly was hidden, so within the first few conferences with a manipulator, you may discover him/her to be a selfless and helpful individual.

11. Guilt Tripping

Pay close attention to a person who regularly attempts to make you experience responsibilities. It is possible that the person is manipulating you.

Manipulators are conscious that different people have an extraordinary sense of right and wrong so that they take advantage of the good nature in their victims to preserve them in the self-doubting, guilt-ridden, tense, and submissive roles.

12. Shaming

In case you catch a person frequently saying insulting remarks or hurtful comments about your weight, own family, appearance or employment, and so forth, then this must be taken as a caution signal—of a manipulative buddy. Manipulators pay close attention to a person's insecurities and weak factors. In case you are insecure about your weight or don't just like the shape of your nostrils, they are quick to be aware. If you have failed an examination again and again, they will make fun of you for it. Our fulfillment or bodily appearance isn't always in our control, so making a laugh of a person's difficult scenario suggests the mean and predatory nature of the character. They frequently attempt to bypass off their offensive remarks as jokes, but in case you pay close attention, your instinct will tell you that the jokes are not humorous and have unfriendly overtones. It's their secret to try to bring you down. What they gain by doing that?

Manipulators use shaming to make their sufferer sense insufficient or unworthy, and consequently, emerge as submissive to them. It's a powerful tactic to create an endured experience of private inadequacy in the sufferer, therefore, permitting the manipulator to maintain a function of dominance.

13. Intimidation

Manipulators usually use covert intimidation. Their threats are carefully veiled. A manipulator may additionally twist the fact to make you doubt your perceptions.

14. Fuel lighting fixtures

Possibly not an early warning signal, however, it's far a powerful tactic used by manipulators. The time owes its foundation to the play fuel light and its movie variations, after which it turned into money. When you consider that, then the time has been utilized in clinical and research literature. It is a way of twisting reality for a particular purpose.

A manipulator is a genius with regards to twisting reality to serve their purposes. It doesn't count number what the reality is, they have got a way of in the end displaying you that it is your fault and that you don't see matters truthfully. By the point you receive their version of the truth, you've got come to be so mentally sick that you can't accept as true with your perceptions.

If a person questions your perceptions of truth, do not trust their opinion.

Always listen to your intuition. What it tells you approximately a person or a situation is right.

15. Rationalization

It is an excuse a manipulative individual gives for engaging in hurtful or beside the point behaviors. It may be an effective tactic, especially when the explanation presented makes simply enough experience that any conscientious person is probable to fall for it.

Rationalization serves three primary purposes:

- It eliminates inner resistance the manipulator might have about their dangerous movement.

- It continues others off their back.

- If the manipulator can persuade you, they are justified in doing what they had been doing, then they're unfastened to pursue their desires.

I once had a pal who would every so often behave very affectionately, however, after a few hours or days might turn out to be very cold. I became unwell of her hot and cold conduct. On every occasion, I'd convey attention to her terrible conduct or I'd avoid her, she might right away feel that and could come to my room crying, telling me how busy and depressed she has been within the past few days. I would be moved with the aid of her tears and forgive her remaining week's terrible conduct, however, after a few days, and she'd repeat the precise awful behavior.

Manipulators are first-rate actors. They can fake to be a sufferer. They can cry a river on every occasion they need. They could fake love. They could fake joy or some other emotion. So carefully study the actions of those who declare to love you or who try to advantage your sympathy by losing tears.

It's noble to be kind and gentle but pick the receivers of your kindness very carefully.

16. Diversion

While you are attempting to keep a discussion focused on single trouble or behavior (that you recall bad or cruel), but a person changes the situation or dodges the issue, then this must warn you.

17. Unsettling Stare

Many people trust that eyes are home windows to the soul. Some people respond to the emotionless stare of a skilled manipulator with soreness, whilst others experience hypnotized through them.

CHAPTER 8
HOW TO ANALYZE AND READ PEOPLE

Here are nine hints for reading human beings:

1. Create a baseline

Humans have distinctive quirks and patterns of behavior. For example, they may clear their throat, study the ground whilst speaking, cross their arms, scratch their head, stroke their neck, squint, pout, or jiggle their toes often. To start with, we might not even observe whilst others do this stuff. If we do, we do not supply it good deal attention.

People show those behaviors for different reasons. They may simply be mannerisms. Occasionally, however, those same actions can be indicative of deception, anger, or anxiety.

Creating an intellectual baseline of others' regular behavior will help you.

2. Search for deviations

Be aware of inconsistencies between the baseline you've got created and the man or woman's phrases and gestures.

For example, have you noticed that an important provider of yours has the dependency of clearing his throat time and again while worried. As he introduces some surprisingly small modifications to your enterprise association, he starts to do this. Is there more right here than meets the attention?

You would decide to probe besides, asking a few extra questions than you will usually have.

3. Be aware clusters of gestures

No single gesture or word always method something, however, while numerous behavioral aberrations are clumped together, observe closely.

For instance, now not simplest does your provider hold clearing his throat; however, he additionally does that head-scratching thing. In addition, he continues shuffling his feet.

Continue with a warning.

4. Compare and evaluation

Adequate, so that you've observed is that a person acting a touch exclusive than normal. Move your statement up a notch to deduce if that character repeats the identical behavior with others in your group.

Keep having a look at the individual as he or she interacts with others inside the room. Does the individual's expression exchange? How about his or her posture and frame language?

5. Check out the mirror

Mirror neurons are integrated video display units in our brains that replicate other people's nation of mind. We're stressed to study each other's body language. A grin activates the smile muscle mass in our very own faces while a frown turns on our frown muscle mass.

Although we see a person we love, our eyebrows arch, facial muscles loosen up, head tilts, and blood flows to our lips, making them full.

In case your accomplice does not reciprocate that conduct, this person could be sending you a clear message: She or he does not, such as you or are not satisfied with something you've got finished.

6. Become aware of the robust voice

The maximum effective person isn't always the one sitting at the head of the desk.

Assured people have robust voices. Around a conference room table, the most confident individual could be the most effective one: Expansive posture, sturdy voice, and a massive smile (Don't confuse a loud voice with a sturdy one).

In case you're pitching an idea to a group, it's clean to take note of the leader of the group, but that leader may additionally have a vulnerable personality. In truth, he or she relies closely on others to make decisions and is without problems stimulated via them.

Discover the strong voice and your possibilities for achievement growth dramatically.

7. Examine how they walk

Normally, individuals who shuffle along with lack a flowing movement in their actions or preserve their head down lack self-belief.

8. Pinpoint movement phrases

As an FBI agent, I found phrases had been the closest manner for me to get into any other individual's head. Phrases constitute thoughts, so perceive the phrase this is freighted with, which means.

For example, if your boss says she's "Decided to go with brand X," the movement word is determined. This unmarried word shows that maximum possibly your boss 1) isn't impulsive, 2) weighed numerous alternatives, and 3) thinks things through.

Action phrases offer insights into the way a person thinks.

9. Look for personality clues

Every folk has a unique character; however, there are fundamental clarifications that will let you relate to every other character so that you can examine her or him appropriately.

- Does someone show more introverted or extroverted behavior?

- Does she or he seem driven by relationships or significance?

- How does the character handle danger and uncertainty?

- What feeds his or her ego?

- What are the person's behaviors while confused?

- What are the person's behaviors while at ease?

CHAPTER 9
A WAY TO COPE WITH PREDATORS?

Concepts That Predators Will Use Against You

Social psychologist Robert Cialdini has examined loads of research approximately compliance and conformity to perceive key objects of human nature is a good way to "Pass someone on your route," and he has delineated six middle standards of the way to persuade others.

He claims that proper persuaders "Strum strings that are interior everybody." He says their intention to create attunement, a kingdom of mind that is prepared for the actions that follow. For example, first ask people if they're beneficial, after which ask for his or her assistance. They'll help due to the fact they need to be consistent with their self-evaluation.

Even though Cialdini urges us to use those standards ethically, i.e., to train and improve, it's not tough to look at how someone with much less lofty desires might make the most of them. In truth, those points of attunement echo psychologist Robert Hare's warnings without a sense of right and wrong about predatory psychopaths. (I just spent five years writing with BTK Killer Dennis Rader, which yielded plenty of scary insights about predatory vigilance.)

To shield yourself, you should begin to recognize how predators can use not unusual human dispositions in opposition to you. The matters that work to get us to agree or conform are identical matters that make us goals.

Permit's examined the six standards and keeps in mind how a predator perspective them:

1. Authority.

We tend to view a person is a function of authority as having know-how or electricity, so we obey. Predators realize what we count on and they offer fake credentials spiked with a robust dose of self-assurance.

2. Reciprocity.

We feel obligated while someone gives us a gift or does us a desire: We need to give back. Hare states that psychopaths will provide gifts or do favors to get a foot within the door. Presents and favors now not handiest obligate, however, they also deflect your attention from the predator's real purpose.

3. Liking.

While we experience comfortable with or tremendous approximately, someone, we tend to say yes to their requests. The perceived similarity makes us sense safer and greater inclined to give a special remedy. Predators use compliments, commonplace interests, and common identification to boom rapport. (Rader did this while he became stopped through a police officer simply after a murder, through playing to their shared focus of a Boy Scout camp, which also gave him the advent of being a nice man.)

4. Shortage.

We place value on items that we accept as vital while they are in short supply or available for only a restricted time. Predators provide suitable items or services within this context, as a hook.

5. Social Evidence.

While we don't recognize what to do in a scenario, we appeal to others to help us determine, clean commands can elicit our cooperation, particularly if its miles offered as a majority preference. Predators look ahead to this sense of uncertainty in us and step in to offer route.

6. Dedication and Consistency.

When we decide to do something, we tend to follow through with it, mainly if we make it publicly known. We need to show that our values outline and direct us. Predators will elicit a small initial commitment to leverage us into a larger one. As soon as we are in, the higher the stakes—and the more we'll behave as they direct. According to Hare, predators disguise their d evil intention until they get us beyond the point in which it's tough to disengage.

Psychopathic predators search for our triggers, so the better we understand our points of vulnerability; the simpler it is for us to malignant manipulation. All of us can be duped, even for the duration of a short interaction, so take some time to ensure that the persuader is proper and offers genuine benefit. Do your studies and get evidence. Don't just let someone strum your strings.

Ways Predators Will Try To Take Advantage And Prey For Your Politeness

Making plans time away from domestic involves packing, training, and belief. Airports and other transportation centers are infamous crook hot spots, capitalizing on distraction, and travelers' loss of discernment. Right here are some hints to beautify attention.

I will begin with a caveat to which many common vacationers will attest: Most fellow travelers are innocent, beneficial, gracious, and kind. Yet this is precisely why we are tempted to extend the benefit of the doubt to folks who are not. This column is about the small percentage of dangerous individuals and a way to spot them. While away from home, be especially aware of those five methods dangerous people would possibly try to ingratiate themselves with you or your own family.

1. Stranded Strangers: "Pressured Teaming."

The concept of "Forced Teaming" is defined by author Gavin de Becker in the countrywide bestseller "The Gift of Worry" as a manipulative method of establishing untimely consideration. A shared predicament frequently stimulates mutual support but may be exploited by predators seeking a socially suitable excuse to invade private situations.

A canceled flight, school classes, or bus experience creates a common floor amongst the ones left stranded. Especially if it's dark or late at night, the stranger who turns to you and asks, "How are we going to get home?" must be regarded with warning. You have not ended up part of a stranger's "We" by mutual misfortune. Even as bonding over a commonplace dilemma can result in cooperation, it no longer automatically requires you to collaborate or share travel plans — particularly with a person who makes you uncomfortable.

2. Etiquette Shaming: Preying Upon Politeness

We are socialized to be gracious and kind. Deviants prey in this social custom, in which politeness attracts predators.

We are widely used to the not very often, "Pardon me, you do not seem to know me. However, I absolutely could use your help/recommendation/money." We're socialized to attend to the wishes of others in all fairness and to concentrate while a stranger civilly speaks to us.

Yet, in case you are on my own, visiting with young youngsters, or in any other case wary of attractive with someone who makes you feel uncomfortable, keep in mind that you aren't obligated to talk to strangers, even less likely to help them do something.

3. Boundary Violations: Too Close For Consolation

Airports and bus stations are crowded. Yet do now not allow a stranger to invade your personal space by sitting too near you or your youngsters due to the fact you fear appearing rude. Many personal space invasions are innocent; however, you can't spot a sex culprit through searching. If someone sits too near your baby, particularly while there are different seats to be had, and right away strikes up a verbal exchange with him or her, move.

4. Strangers Grew To Become Stalkers: Buddies, Fans, and Fans

Last century before the internet, human beings experienced the "Strangers on a whim" phenomenon — feeling comfortable sharing intimate info with a stranger at the same time as journeying whom they never predicted to see again. If you did this these days, you will at once pick out up a new Facebook pal and Twitter follower. In addition, perhaps have the selfie you took together tagged, flagged, and retweeted as quickly as your conversation ends. Moreover, due to the fact, all of the content material published by using your new pal/fan/follower (stranger) may have your name and present-day vicinity, make sure you have been honest because you are not in the workplace.

Again, they are the exception to the guideline, I have personally handled a great variety of stalking instances that started with the friendly verbal exchange between strangers. While hanging up casual communications on public transportation, ensure you recognize approximately enough your seatmate before you expose yourself. Furthermore, do not feel bad about declining to show a curious stranger your call or private number, or social media just in case you are uncomfortable with the request. Polite conversation is feasible without oversharing.

5. Likability is a trap

Be wary of strangers who approach your toddler to offer for help or instructions. Most parents view this as a notoriously obvious ploy to access victims. On the other hand, some predators are so polished and practiced of their craft, they lower defenses through likability — attractive to parents and children alike. In addition, consider that rapport-building professions of similarity together with "My son is the same age as yours" aren't genuine.

Even though reminding your family about stranger risk and discussing sexual attack prevention is by no means fine, information is energy. The attention of the approaches where predators assume and behave will enhance your capability to spot red flags and continue with warning.

CHAPTER 10
ETHICAL USE OF DARK PSYCHOLOGY FOR SUCCESS IN DAILY EXISTENCE

How Psychology Can Improve Your Life?

How can psychology apply to your everyday life? Do you believe that psychology is just for students, academics, and therapists? Then think again! Due to the fact, psychology is both a practicable action and theoretical research, it can be utilized in a variety of the methods.

At the same time, as studies research isn't precisely mild reading cloth for the common man or woman, the results of these experiments and research may have sizeable applications in daily life. The following are some of the top ten realistic uses for psychology in regular life:

1. Get Prompted

Whether your purpose is to stop smoking, lose weight, or examine a new language, some training from psychology provides pointers for buying motivated. To grow your motivation while drawing close a project, make use of some of the subsequent tips derived from research in cognitive and educational psychology:

- Introduce new or novel factors to hold your interest high.

- Vary the series to help stave off boredom.

- Study new matters that build on your present understanding.

- Set clear goals that might be at once related to the assignment.

2. Enhance Your Management Abilities

It doesn't count number in case you're an office supervisor or a volunteer at a neighborhood teenage activity group, having true leadership abilities will in all likelihood, be vital sometime in the future for your existence. Now, not all of us is a born leader, but some easy suggestions taken from mental studies can help you improve your leadership capabilities.

One of the most famous research papers on this topic looked at three distinct management styles. Primarily based on the findings of this look at and subsequent studies, practice several the following when you are in a management function:

- Offer clear steering but permit group contributors to voice opinions.

- Communicate approximately possible answers to troubles with contributors to the group.

- Focus on stimulating ideas and be inclined to praise creativity.

3. Come To Be A Better Communicator

Conversation involves a whole lot more than just the way you speak or write. Research indicates that nonverbal indicators make up a big portion of our interpersonal communications. To communicate your message successfully, you want to learn how to express yourself nonverbally and to study the nonverbal cues of those around you.

Some key strategies encompass the subsequent:

- Use proper eye contact.

- Start noticing nonverbal indicators in others.

- Learn to use your tone of voice to boost your message.

4. Learn To Better Understand Others

Just like nonverbal communication, your capacity to apprehend your emotions and the feelings of those around you perform an important role in your relationships and professional lifestyles. The time emotional intelligence refers to your potential to apprehend each of your emotions in addition to those of other human beings.

Your emotional intelligence quotient is a measure of this potential. Consistent with psychologist Daniel Goleman, your EQ may be more crucial than your IQ.

What can you do to emerge as more emotionally stable? Recall a few the subsequent techniques:

- Cautiously assess your very own emotional reactions.

- Record your enjoyment and emotions in a

journal.

- Try to see situations from the angle of a different person.

5. Make Extra Correct Selections

Studies in cognitive psychology supply a wealth of statistics about choice making. By making use of those techniques for your lifestyles, you can discover ways to make wiser choices. The following time you want to make a huge decision, strive the usage of several the subsequent techniques:

- Try using the "Six Thinking Hats" technique with the aid of searching on the situation from multiple points of view, including rational, emotional, intuitive, creative, advantageous, and Dark views.

- Recall the capacity prices and blessings of choice.

- Appoint a grid evaluation approach that offers a score for how a selected decision will fulfill unique requirements you may have.

6. Enhance Your Reminiscence

Have you ever wondered why you can remember the precise information of childhood events yet forget the call of the new customer you met yesterday? Research on how we form new reminiscences as well as how and why we forget has caused some of the findings that can be implemented without delay in your daily life.

What are some methods you can grow your reminiscence of electricity?

- Awareness of the data.

- Rehearse what you have discovered.

- Do away with distractions.

7. Make Wiser financial decisions

Nobel Prize-winning psychologist Daniel Kahneman and his colleague Amos Tversky performed a chain of research that looked at how humans manipulate uncertainty and danger while making decisions. The next studies in this area, referred to as behavioral economics has yielded some key findings that you may use to make wiser money management choices.

One looks at located that workers could extra than triple their financial savings by making use of some of the following strategies:

- Don't procrastinate. Start investing savings now.

- Commit earlier to dedicate quantities of your future profits in your retirement financial savings.

- Try to be aware of non-public biases that may result in Dark money choices.

8. Get Higher Grades

The subsequent time you are tempted to whine about pop quizzes, midterms, or finals, consider that research has confirmed that taking checks honestly helps you better consider what you have learned, even if it wasn't on the test.

Every other study discovered that repeated check-taking might be a higher reminiscence aid than studying. College students who were tested again and again have been able to remember 61% of the content while the ones within the have a look at group recalled most effective

40%. How can you observe those findings to your lifestyles? While seeking to research new data, self-check frequently to cement what you have learnt, into your memory.

9. Become More Effective

Occasionally, it looks as if there are hundreds of books, blogs, and magazine articles telling us the way to get more completed in an afternoon. However, how much of this advice is based on real studies? As an example, think about the variety of times have you ever heard that multitasking can help you become more productive. Studies have discovered that trying to carry out multiple missions at the same time severely impairs pace, accuracy, and productiveness.

What classes from psychology can you operate to boom your productivity? Consider several the following:

- Avoid multitasking while running on complex or dangerous obligations.

- Cognizance at the venture at hand.

- Eliminate distractions.

10. Be Healthier

Psychology also can be a useful device for improving your ordinary health. From approaches to encourage workout and better nutrients to new remedies for melancholy, the sector of fitness psychology gives a wealth of beneficial strategies that can help you to be more healthy and happier.

Some examples that you may practice at once in your very own existence:

- Research has shown that both daylight and synthetic mild can reduce the symptoms of seasonal affective sickness.

- Studies have demonstrated that exercise can contribute to more mental well-being.

- Studies have determined that supporting people apprehend the dangers of bad behaviors can lead to healthier choices.

CHAPTER 11

BONUS REALISTIC POINTERS ON HANDLING & THE USE OF DARK PSYCHOLOGY/ THOUGHTS HINTS

You now recognize the principle ideas behind dark psychology and the way these ideas are carried out in an expansion of conditions. That is effective, however, on its personal, no longer enough. By taking the time to learn about dark psychology through the evaluation of real international case studies, you will see the ideas in this eBook delivered to lifestyles.

The case studies also are eye catching, charming memories. They offer an insight into several the most psychologically rare types of people this planet has ever produced.

Each case has a look at is laid out in a manner that is as beneficial as possible for a budding disciple of dark psychology. Real records regarding each case look at is supplied earlier than psychological perception is extracted and simplified. Each case observes they will then be immediately related to the Dark psychology determined in this eBook to assist you to recognize it in a richer and greater meaningful manner.

The instances contained in this chapter are the most extreme examples of dark psychology during human history. They may be provided not to be glorified or even judged, but rather learned from.

Instructions From records' Narcissistic Dictators

Statistics

One of the textbook trends of narcissists is their view of their very own reputation and self-worth as some distance above anything genuinely justified by reality. This commonly leads to people with an inflated ego being trapped in lifestyles and conditions that they see as essentially under them. Every so often, a person with a narcissistic personality is born right into a situation where they have got the strength and status to express their narcissism. Nothing exemplifies this extra than some of the records' dictators who had the electricity and manipulate to fit their egos. Some of their tales are offered right here.

Saparmurat Niyazov is one of the fine examples of a narcissist having the possibility to meet grandiose inclinations. He took over as chief of Turkmenistan and was able to take gain of a power vacuum left through the crumble of Soviet ideology. His ascent from leader to the pure manifestation of narcissism started when he determined he needs to be President for the lifestyles of Turkmenistan. From there, total electricity brought about some memorably narcissistic selections.

One of the greater infamous aspects of Niyazov's rule turned into the renaming of the months of the year to reflect his non-public glory. He carried out bizarrely precise legal guidelines in accordance together with his non-public whims, consisting of proscribing residents' appearance and renaming commonplace everyday gadgets according to what he felt they need to be called.

Perhaps the most effective instance of Niyazov's grandiosity became his manufacturing of a non-secular textual content that became given equal repute within the United States as established scriptures, such as The Holy

Qur'an. Different dictators, along with Colonel Gaddafi of Libya, have produced further "Respected" texts. That is an acknowledged trait, perhaps exceptional evidenced through the repute afforded to Adolf Hitler's "Mein Kampf" within Nazi Germany.

A better-regarded, but equally terrifying, the dynasty of dictators is that of the leaders of North Korea. Cutting-edge dictator Kim Jong Un and his father Kim Jong Il are afforded the repute of deities inside their tightly controlled nation, and this is pondered within the "Facts" that North Korean citizens are furnished about their lives.

What can such outlandish examples educate us approximately narcissism? Many of the tendencies exhibited by way of such dictators are examples of how controlling and pedantic narcissists emerge as whilst granted enough electricity to carry out their wishes.

For example, a permit takes North Korea. The modern dictator, Kim Jong Un, is reported to have had his uncle carried out for yawning in an assembly. The technique of execution - An anti-aircraft weapon can destroy fighter jets. That is an instance of the narcissist's want for flattery and anger when not receiving it taken to its logical end.

The various times of dictators producing non-secular, spiritual, or philosophical treatises, which are then accelerated to the fame of required, sanctified analyzing inside us of a is an instance of the narcissistic idea of being "Unique" and "Same to humanity's greatest figures." In narcissists' minds, they may be the contemporaries of prophets and saints and rare breeds. If you could hold close the amount to which they surely believe this to be the case, then their book of such egotistical texts starts evolved to make a twisted kind of feel.

Hitler - The Present-day Machiavelli

Data

Many parallels may be drawn among the political thoughts of Machiavelli, as expressed through "The Prince," and the political career of Adolf Hitler. The argument can consequently be made that Hitler is the satisfactory feasible illustration of what a real cutting-edge Machiavellian chief seems like. We will first look at the similarities among Hitler's thoughts and deeds and those of Machiavelli, before exploring the insights into Machiavellianism as a trait that Hitler gives.

One of the first similarities that may be drawn between Machiavelli and Hitler is the assertion in "The Prince" that peace ought to most effectively be visible as a brief respite in an in no way-ending conflict. Hitler becomes committed to conquest and deliberate to, in the end, take over the complete global beneath his totalitarian 1/3 Reich. Hitler is, therefore, the nearest aspect the cutting-edge world has visible to Machiavelli's idea of a ceaseless warrior ruler.

Machiavelli changed into additionally an endorsement of making and manipulating the truth to sort a predetermined political intention. Infamously, one among Hitler's center doctrines was the persecution and next extermination of Germany's Jewish populace. One of the key activities that helped Hitler pursue this genocidal purpose was the fake flag operation referred to as the Reichstag fire.

It is a matter of dialogue whether Hitler engineered this event to fit his anti-Jewish and anti-Communist agenda, but a huge body of evidence suggests he did exactly that. Regardless of the exact circumstance, the incident is a powerful example of a Machiavellian false flag tactic getting used to serving some other intention entirely.

One of the key thoughts behind Machiavelli's political concept and next Machiavellian people is that electricity is a worthy stop intention in and of itself. Irrespective of what strategies are used to preserve directly and hold strength, they are justified in line with Machiavelli's blueprint of how a frontrunner must behave.

Hitler is a textbook example of this concept in motion. Hitler knew how to manipulate the political system of the time as well as the hearts and minds of the German humans. There's a strong suggestion that Hitler may also have escaped Nazi Germany and fled to Argentina to stay out the relaxation of his days surrounded by fellow Nazi escapees. That is tough to prove both manners; however, it is a manageable illustration of never letting go of energy, even in the face of apparent demise.

Records have given that world battle two has painted Hitler because of the epitome and embodiment of evil, the closest aspect the Earth has ever visible to an incarnation of Satan. At the time, even though, Hitler changed into similarly adept at triggering responses of love and worry.

One desires most effective to look at the video of Hitler's speeches to show the combination of awe and terror Hitler becomes able to initiate.

One of the key Machiavellian thoughts to emerge from "The Prince" is the precept of not keeping your phrase, your promise if it isn't always in your interest to achieve this. Machiavelli emphasizes the want to, as a minimum; appear to be straightforward, regardless of what the truth of the scenario may be.

Hitler gives a true insight into how actual-global figures with political strength can carry out this concept. One trademark function of Hitler's speeches changed into that they delivered epic and hard-to-put into effect promises that might in no way realistically reach fruition. Although Hitler turned into now able to deliver on the thoughts he put forward in his rhetoric. He controlled to maintain the image of being a person striving to supply on his word. That is a clear real-global instance of the Machiavellian concept of setting apart reality and public perception to effective mental effect.

Any other Machiavellian concept exemplified with the aid of Hitler became the consolidation of strength and the elimination of threats. Hitler systematically removed everybody who opposed his quest to guide Germany returned to its former glory. He removed virtually all of us who stood in his manner—former allies, holders of rival ideologies, or ethnic companies Hitler felt the want to rid Germany of. This concentration of strength caused Hitler to be capable of exercising as a great deal to have an impact on as he did. This suggests that the Machiavellian idea is powerful in exercise, even inside the current era.

A very last perception provided by using Hitler into the world of dark psychology is his use of, and exuberance for, sadism. This zone of the dark Tetrad is particularly obvious inside the manner Hitler dealt with those compelled into his concentration camps. The fates of those bad souls protected torture, scientific experimentation, and demise with the aid of hunger or gassing.

Brainwashing - How Terrorists Control Minds?

Facts

One of the predominant examples of brainwashing

getting used inside the modern era is by terrorist groups. Many human beings will count on this indicates Islamist extremists, such as Al Qaeda and ISIS, but in fact, terrorists exist across the political spectrum. Violent terrorists are probably influenced through their spiritual beliefs or sturdy political affairs originating from both the proper and the left of the spectrum. What all those numerous businesses proportion, however, is their use of brainwashing strategies to recruit and maintain followers.

The power of such brainwashing cannot be overvalued. International locations from throughout the Western globe are dropping their younger humans to terrorists running inside the center East. How are such overseas groups able to attract so strongly? They are by the usage of planned, carefully controlled brainwashing procedures.

One specific issue particular to the present-day global of brainwashing is the terrorists' use of the internet to support their objectives and ideologies. Historically, brainwashing frequently needed to occur in a bodily context of proximity, which includes in a cult headquarters or a few regions comparable. Way to the internet, terror organizations can reach out and speak to people, irrespective of in which inside the global they stay. The high-definition propaganda movies launched through companies are any other device inside the new, high-tech world of brainwashing and indoctrination.

Although the cutting-edge international of terrorist associated brainwashing capabilities factors in no way before seen, it also uses the tried-and-examined indoctrination methodologies which have been around for decades. The ideas at the back of brainwashing are the same as they have ever been—the terrorist businesses are just making use of them in technologically revolutionary methods.

The severity of this problem can't be exaggerated. A way to the untraceably reach terrorist companies through the net, no country or circle of relatives is safe from the ability brainwashing that tragically happens so often. This can involve younger people with their entire lives in advance of them, leaving behind their acquainted world to journey and die in a foreign struggle. It could also encourage mentally deranged people to carry out "Lone Wolf" attacks on their communities and countries.

The current use of brainwashing methods conducted through the internet affords an application of traditional standards up to date for the contemporary global. Finding vulnerable sufferers is possibly less complicated than ever before than for individuals who desire to indoctrinate others. Way to the social norm of younger human beings sharing their lives online, it is straightforward for almost every person, no matter who they are or what intentions they have, to tune down a goal to be vulnerable to terror's insidious effect on.

Way to the paintings of undercover newshounds undertaking sting operations, we've got an extraordinary insight into the contemporary situation regarding the brainwashing strategies utilized by terror companies. After a victim has been recognized, they'll normally be assigned to one member of the fear institution who it's far felt might be capable of speak with them in an effective and influential way.

In line with traditional brainwashing concepts, the newly assigned recruiter will start to work on their goal slowly and methodically. Whatever objectionable that the terror institution represents can be hidden from sight till the victim has displayed a whole lot of willingness and open-mindedness concerning potentially polarizing ideas.

Many modern terror groups use the attempted-and-tested approach of imparting their ideology as a utopian way to the specific non-public woes of the target. Regardless of whether the terror organization occurs to be selling Islamic extremism or proper-wing racism, their processes are greater or much less the equal. They like to push a story of a society that has long past wrong and their proposed answer as the only answer to restoration it. Such convincing portrayals are aided by way of the video and photograph skills of the net, which permit groups to position across a heavily biased model of life inside their ideology.

Like conventional brainwashing, cutting-edge terrorist efforts go away a sufferer feeling as though they may be fortunate and fortunate to have come into touch with the terrorist agency. Infinite examples exist of younger people with plenty to stay for who, after being in prolonged contact with a terrorist brainwasher, emerge as expressing feelings of thank you and advantages for

"Coming Across" their new appearance on life.

It is a mistake to anticipate that modern terror groups and their brainwashing efforts are solely focused on the net. This isn't always the case. Terrorists and different ideological extremists see the net as one device among many they can use. The quit aim of maximum businesses is still to make bodily touch with the character and make them an offline a part of their global as nicely. It is frequently whilst the sufferer moves into offline contact with the organization that the severity of the brainwashing will increase rapidly.

Modern-day terror agencies are frequently aware that the utopian imaginative and prescient they've painted online will be unexpectedly uncovered as patently false once the recruit spends some time many of the institutions in person. For this reason, such businesses are frequently brief to stress the victim into organizing roots in the new international that they have chosen. This often involves marrying any other member of the company. Forming such near bonds to the group's offline activities enables them to keep recruits enslaved, even after the utopian best is uncovered as fantasy.

170

Rasputin - Black Magic or Dark Psychology?

Records

No series of case studies on Dark psychology would be whole without an exam of Rasputin and all that the notorious "Mad Monk" represents. Rasputin is an exciting determine as the form of mental strength he wielded echoed a long way into the future and stimulated many elements of charismatic influencers that appeared later.

Who precisely was Rasputin? He became a non-secular determine who was able to gain impact over the ruling Russian elite of his era. Rasputin controlled to undertaking an intoxicating blend of piousness and sensuality that appealed to nearly any aspect of a person Rasputin wanted it to. Folks who were willing to be motivated by using religion were without difficulty inspired through the monk's apparent powers of healing. Those who preferred the sensual pleasures of the sector discovered a lot to respect in Rasputin's man or woman in that regard also.

Many elements of Rasputin's dark mental have an

impact on also can be in subsequent aspects of hypnosis. Rasputin is one of the earliest and maximum infamous figures who became able to set off something just like a trancelike state of suggestibility inside the minds and souls of his sufferers.

What exactly had been the "Hypnotic" and "Restoration" powers Rasputin was rumored to have? It was said that Rasputin turned into capable of set-off deep feelings of calm, ease, and rest in his victims. He became a forerunner to trendy religious healers in lots of methods. Memories of his capabilities to ease the aches and pains of the Russian the Aristocracy introduced to his mystique and the amount of impact he turned into capable of having on almost all people around him.

Rasputin also relates to some of the ideas observed within the area of covert emotional manipulation. One of the reasons that the impact of Rasputin was so high-quality and infamous turned into that he in no way seemed to be trying to manipulate his sufferers. Alternatively, it truly got here throughout that he had some type of inexplicable "Energy" and "Aura" that human beings succumbed to. You may probably recognize those emotions as hallmarks of what we term "Covert emotional manipulation" within the current context.

The case has a look at Rasputin is applicable for college students of charismatic have an impact on. Inside the current context, many dark psychological manipulators can entice followers due to the belief that they possess some sort of special or secret understanding.

This precept was even more effective within the time of Rasputin. The sector changed into much less rational and technology became a much less evolved. This gave greater credence to the perception of Rasputin as divine and mystically effective. College students of psychology can be without problems capable of draw parallels among the energy of this supernatural portrayal and comparable charismatic leaders of the current international who feign spirituality as a manner of gaining influence and manage.

The link between psychological energy and sexual expression is also clear with Rasputin. Like limitless others for the duration of history, he leveraged his psychological knowledge to have an impact on into a life of promiscuity and decadent indulgence. It's no twist of fate that cult leaders across the world are often found enjoying their preference of followers, bodily talking. Rasputin is an infamous instance of this precept; however, he's by no means the first individual to place it into practice.

The CIA Desires You To Kill Humans - MKUltra Information

The reality that this example has a look at even exists is surprising. When we communicate approximately MKUltra, what is it we are discussing? No less than the CIA's own extended and extreme attempts to recognize and increase thoughts-manage techniques. This can sound like the ramblings of a paranoid character sporting a tinfoil hat, but it's far from it. Conduct your studies into MKUltra and you will see that the program changed into very real and intense experience. By getting to know classes from it, we can see that even the most "Civilized" countries understand the strength of brainwashing and attempt to use it for their ends.

If the concept of a mystery CIA program is into thoughts manipulate tough to believe, then the info of this system even more so. The CIA attempted to develop, test, and apprehend a huge range of mind-manipulate techniques, inclusive of the physical ones, which include sleep deprivation, the ones which might be psychological, which includes identification erasing, and those which can be pharmaceutical, along with "Reality Serums" and other pills.

At least research software of this type might have been performed inside the most proper and moral manner viable, right? Wrong. The program was illegal and unethical. How unethical? The management of LSD and different materials to unwitting and unknowing U.S. citizens was an indicator of this system.

Several the unproven elements of the MKUltra application are the maximum traumatic of all. A concept exists which states that the CIA turned into able to hypnotically lead a man, Sirhan, into assassinating a member of the Kennedy own family. Credible witnesses, consisting of psychologists, state that Sirhan was surely working below some form of hypnotic impact all through the homicide itself and the subsequent trial segment. Sirhan has stated he has no recollection of whatever that befell and cannot consider, making statements he is on the original document.

The CIA's use of thoughts manages strategies and research into their effectiveness has helped to pave the manner for some distance more valid current techniques of influence. For example, MKUltra made pioneering use of mixing pills and mental techniques to exert an influence on a target. A few modern-day psychologists can use this mixture in an extra tremendous manner to treat mental disorders in place of only to manipulate and manage.

Curiously, MKUltra also shines mild upon how Machiavellian tactics of political influence are alive and well even in present day-day us. The USA regularly portrays itself as a very ethical country that isn't organized to compromise on its values of freedom and equality. What MKUltra without a doubt demonstrates is that the CIA is inclined to take the Machiavellian approach of doing one component publicly and any other component privately. Whilst the CIA decided it become in its pastimes to achieve this, it became willing to check risky psychedelic pills on American citizens without their consent or knowledge.

If the elements of Sirhan's involvement in MKUltra are ever established, then terrifying possibilities come to be obvious. Such proof could confirm, beyond a shadow of a doubt that hypnotism can be used to directly affect a person to perform an assassination. Some modern-day-day tries to verify those techniques or disproving them have already been made. Contemporary-day hypnotist Derren Brown claims to have replicated the impact of MKUltra; however, this declaration can be down to a few other forms of illusion on behalf of Brown.

The Psychological Secrets of Con Artists

Information

The truth that "Con Artists" are recognized by the second one a part of their name is a testament to the extent of dark mental skill they possess. Cutting-edge mental researchers frequently express a deep degree of surprise that many con artists have traditionally operated in step with ideas of having an impact on that has simplest lately been proved by cutting-edge science. There's a clear indication that many of the records' most infamous con artists had been Dark mental masters with a mastery of ideas the present-day world is only just starting to comprehend.

Have you ever heard of a Ponzi scheme? The call is taken from a person, Charles Ponzi, who changed into able to behavior a big scale fraudulent investment scheme. One of the most relevant examples of this unique Ponzi scheme is Charles's willingness to apply the energy of projection and portrayal of his very own confidence to get out of sticky conditions. For example, Charles once had a collection of indignant buyers arrive at his workplace. Rather than panicking, as many people could, Charles became able to remain calm and collected, and placate the mob through his tranquil, inspiring demeanor.

Faith healers share a few similarities with Charles Ponzi insofar as they prey on their victims' vulnerability to serve their objectives. While Ponzi made use of his sufferers' desperation for money and monetary success, religion healers take the more deplorable technique of exploiting a person's sickness and misery, coupled with their victim's choice for a non-secular enjoy, to control them.

The ramifications of encountering a fraudulent religion healer can be very serious indeed. Many tales exist of people who have believed they were healed due to contact with a faith healer. As a result of this obvious restoration, they stop taking medication or do something else medically volatile as a show of accepting as true with and belief. Lamentably, human beings have died from taking those paths.

Every other infamous con artist from the pages of history is Gregor MacGregor. He is the simplest of the earliest acknowledged examples of a person promoting matters that don't exist to wealthy people. When you have ever heard the stories of con artists selling landmarks like the Eiffel Tower or Brooklyn Bridge to naive oldsters with wealth, Gregor MacGregor is the Godfather of this type of con.

MacGregor operated by way of insisting he changed into the Aristocracy from a set of islands that did now not exist. He might recruit people with wealth to fund expeditions to these islands, understanding complete nicely they weren't there. This is exciting, but how precisely is it a precious case looks at in dark psychology?

The cause there may be so much interest in MacGregor is that he became so convincing to his sufferers and knew a way to work their egos and psyches to a detailed and thorough volume that even when they had tried to visit nonexistent islands, they defended MacGregor in the press! That is indicative of MacGregor's advanced psychological manipulation skills.

There are many lessons on Dark psychology to be found out from the con artists. Their capacity to psychologically have an impact on different people is such that even modern-day mental researchers have expressed amazement on the quantity to which con men made use of modern-day psychological findings earlier than they had been showing through technological know-how.

The case of Ponzi indicates the importance of locating a vulnerable victim, ruthlessly exploiting that vulnerability, and doing so in a manner that betrays no doubt or hesitation in any way. Ponzi is a textbook example of a way to increase the probability of a fraud working out by coming across as confident, in control, and unworried always. It is also illustrative of the idea that the great con artists can hold their scams going for decades without being uncovered.

Faith healers offer insight into the suggestibility of the minds of sufferers. Those healers are convincing to the masses that their sufferers made destructive scientific decisions or even died as a result. Religion healers also display why so many people are prone to the effects of charismatic religious cults. While a sturdy spiritual notion is mixed with an actual world want, such as the want to find comfort from a disorder, people may be driven to extreme measures.

Finally, MacGregor offers a laugh perception into the power of using humans' egos against them. Despite the reality that his wealthy traders were exploited financially, had their time wasted, and been made to look silly inside the procedure, however, they selected to publicly defend MacGregor!

What is the lesson we can take from all of this? If a sufferer is found who has an excessive reputation and an inflated opinion of themselves, they're not likely to confess they were tricked or conned. They may now not even admit the actual country of occasions within their thoughts! Interestingly, that is an instance of the way a person's narcissism may be used towards them!

Heavenly Psychopaths - A Soldier's Secrets and Techniques

Statistics

As the time "Psychopath" became general inside the subject of psychology, in addition, in the famous creativeness, it has been associated with negativity. One of the earliest high-profile psychologists, Bowlby, connected the concept to deprivation of maternal interest during youth and said that such humans might generally develop up to be delinquent criminals who have been a burden on society.

Andy McNab is an interesting example of someone with psychopathic developments which many would see as an "Exact Psychopath" if this type of element exists. McNab became abandoned as a toddler and fell right into a lifestyle of petty crime before joining the army as a younger guy. He went directly to rise through the ranks and join Britain's elite SAS (Special Air Service) Special Forces unit. In view that was retiring from the arena of the armed forces; McNab must turn out to be a hit author, playwright, and entrepreneur.

Dr. Dutton is a leading British psychological researcher. He collaborated on an eBook with McNab that explored the idea that psychopathic developments had been virtually beneficial in some conditions. This concept is incredibly revolutionary as it explores the positive implications and advantages of an element of dark psychology that is commonly aligned.

Dutton and McNab had been able to identify some fields in which they felt the Dark psychological trends bestowed through psychopathy could lead to a sensible benefit. One example is all and sundry who must reply to an emergency disaster. Most normal people are not going to carry out in addition to psychopaths. This is due to the presence of fear of their thoughts inflicting doubt and hesitation in their movement. McNab was able to explain that, for a psychopath, it's possible to dial down the fear response at will. This permits psychopaths to operate lightly amid conditions that would be too overwhelming for the general public to handle.

High-threat financial fields, such as hedge fund

control are any other vicinity that McNab and Dutton recognized as being suitable for psychopaths. One function of psychopathy is impulsivity; this permits for risky decisions to be made with little hesitation or fear. In the incorrect context, this could cause murders being executed without a 2D concept, and however, within the proper context, this can result in millions being made on the economic markets.

Their collaboration is extraordinarily useful to the arena of Dark psychology because it combines the theoretical understanding of a researcher with the realistic experience and firsthand anecdotes of a real psychopath who has used their developments to get beforehand within the world in a couple of areas.

This suggests the way that the Dark trait of psychopathy manifests in any given individual is essentially dependent on the situations in which they find themselves. If a person is born with psychopathy and additionally lacks blessings and possibilities, they're vulnerable to end up a risky individual, such as Ted Bundy. If a psychopath is capable of channel their urges into a career this is appropriate for them, and then they may be much more likely to grow to be a conventional success in existence, along with Andy McNab.

Statistics

In an earlier segment of this eBook, we explored the concept of hypnotism as something that exists and can be used by practitioners of Dark psychology to influence the ones around them. NLP (Neuro-Linguistic Programming) is one of the principal techniques that hypnotists use to influence others. The technique is charming and worth knowing approximately. A case has a look at one in every one of its co-creators, Richard Bandler, who offers deep insight into the idea of hypnotic impact and other regions of dark psychology.

Richard Bandler is a debatable character. Moreover, a textbook instance of the way customers of dark psychology is capable of portraying one picture in their existence while the actual truth can be something completely special. Allow's discover this dichotomy.

On the one hand, Richard Bandler claims a wide range of awesome therapeutic achievements, consisting of the use of his very own strategies to no longer want a wheelchair and curing patients which include schizophrenics with unconventional and modern techniques that had been brushed off out of hand by using the world of mainstream psychology. Due to those achievements, many people who do now not know enough about Bandler, assume him to be a moderate-mannered, grandfatherly type who lives and breathes positivity.

The real reality about Bandler is a lot more complicated than one would first anticipate. He grew up in abusive environments in which he becomes physically abused by using a sequence of various person men. In addition, he lives in violation of a few of the things he regularly claims his techniques can fix in someone's life.

As an instance, Bandler claims his NLP and different similar strategies he has worked on can cure someone of the awful and unhealthy habits that plague their existence. No matter what, Bandler smoked cigarettes for decades. Cigarettes were a long way from his simplest vice. Bandler is a publicly admitted past user of cocaine, an exciting trait for a famous public hypnotist.

Possibly the darkest and most intriguing incident from

Bandler's historical past is the murder trial he confronted. What is undisputed is that a lady was shot using Bandler's gun. Bandler became cleared of the crime and insisted that his cocaine supplier used his gun to perform the killing. Whilst reminiscing about the incident, Bandler is much more likely to touch upon the time it took for the jury to clear his name rather than the gravity and severity of the incident itself.

Bandler's use of narcotics is interesting as he isn't the most effective high-profile figure in the discipline of psychology to do so. Sigmund Freud, the originator of current psychoanalysis, became an avid cocaine user genuinely and insisted it was suitable for therapeutic use. These men are textbook examples of how pioneers in the field of dark psychology are unlikely to be constrained by using the rules of society and, as a substitute, decide what is and is not proper for their personal lives.

Many insights into the sector of Dark psychology in fashionable and hypnotism mainly, can be taken from the case , look at Richard Bandler. Possibly the highest placing component of his person and lifestyles is his capability to inspire unique reactions in people. Some people are extraordinarily committed to him and volunteer massive quantities of their time and money to spend time around him. Others view him as one of the most dangerous human beings within the world—a drug person mixed up in homicide who occurs to possess some of the strongest powers to ever be witnessed.

One thing that is sure regarding Richard Bandler, is the grasp of the NLP concept of a reframe. While he is asked about his use of cocaine he's quick to factor out that he becomes more addicted to foods like sweet and peanuts and insists they have been virtually worse for his health! Taking a look at the beginning, this insistence suggests how Bandler can make a severe situation into a lighthearted, even rational scenario through using a comparative reframe.

However, dig deeper and you may realize that Bandler's cocaine provider killed someone, the use of Bandler's gun, and Bandler stood trial for this murder. No matter the severity of this case and the fact it concerned a lack of human lifestyles, Bandler can relate cocaine to the likes of peanuts.

The story of Bandler is also a great example of how

skilled hypnotists and customers of NLP, can manipulate the focus of the man or woman they're manipulating. Bandler frequently manages to explicit his disdain for questions about his non-public life, insisting that he has helped thousands of people through the years and this is not noted in choose of his vices. This argument also seems reasonable before everything glance, but it loses its appeal once the fact of Bandler's smoking, drug use, and the sick-tempered parting of ways along with his NLP co-writer is remembered.

Some other area of Dark psychology that Bandler is possibly the master of, is subtle thought manipulation. Countless examples exist of Bandler's sufferers who declare to have had lifestyles-converting stories interacting with him that they don't recognize, don't recollect, and can't explain. To have this type of profound impact on individuals without giving directly any idea whatsoever of what's taken region is a signature feature of undetected mind manage. All of us who doubt the electricity, or lifestyles, of this approach, desire best to do not forget the electricity of Bandler and the infinite testimonies that tell tales of his mastery.

Facts

In the early chapters of this book, we explored how cults use brainwashing techniques is preferred to draw new participants. We can now take a look at a few case studies of unique cults and the strategies they use to benefit insight into the methods brainwashing is applied to suit the timetable of a specific institution.

The Ku Klux Klan, or KKK, is a secretive white supremacist organization that is underground following its prominence in previous days. Recruiters for the KKK generally tend to apply classic brainwashing technique adopted for his or her very own ambitions and goals. By way of looking at their utilization of those strategies, we will see how the process may be adapted to match a bespoke agenda.

Like any brainwashing, the KKK's begins by way of finding a suitable goal to brainwash. This can often be a younger white male who is down on his luck. A few common targets for the organization include men who've recently misplaced their jobs or skilled a few different forms of misfortune.

The KKK recruiter will begin with begin through warding off any point out of the institution. They'll truly reach out to the goal under the guise of an involved buddy and neighbor who desires to help in a time of need. Slowly, the KKK recruiter will discover the grievances that their goal has and start to relate those to different races. If the recruit had misplaced their process, for instance, the recruiter would slowly start to ensure the recruit linked this to the presence of different races in America.

The KKK recruitment manner is a clear example of how cults and extremist political businesses frequently are similar in their nature and the manner they use brainwashing to attract recruits. The human beings Temple in Jonestown was every other example of how cults regularly have a magical measurement that draws followers and reasons them to carry out excessive acts.

Jim Jones became a charismatic cult chief who controlled to amass land, electricity, and impact to a terrifying volume. Simply as the KKK blurs the traces between a cult, political organization, and terrorist organization, Jonestown was a group that featured a combination of extreme left-wing politics, messianic obedience to Jones, and vague non-secular notions including suicide and reincarnation.

The techniques of Jim Jones are, but every other testament to the power of graduality inside the brainwashing system. Jones could start with benefitting the interest of possible recruiters with the aid of exploring what appeared like rational political ideas and judging their assistance for alternative standards, consisting of the Soviet system. Initiates to the agency slowly surrendered their sanity and freedom, main up to the surprising very last act inside the group's loss of life.

Jonestown ended in a manner that is tragically commonplace to cults—mass suicide. After imploring his followers to perform a political assassination, Jones led his company in a mass suicide. Mothers administered poisoned Kool-useful resources to their toddlers and Jones himself put a bullet through his head. Jonestown is a clear caution of the intense threat that dark psychology represents. Whilst paranoid, charismatic leaders are granted autonomy and manipulate over others, and this is mixed with an excessive stage of isolation from wider society, it could result in totally impossible results, including the mass poisoning of babies.

One of the most surprising and well-known examples of the electricity of isolation to persuade someone to carry out the ambitions of a collection is the case of Patty Hearst. Hearst grew up in a well-known and revered circle of relatives earlier than being abducted via a cultish political fringe group referred to as the SLA.

The kidnapping and subsequent occasions surrounding Hearst are testimony to the strategies of brainwashing in action. At some stage in the kidnapping itself, she adopted into violent behavior for survival. After being taken to the headquarters of the SLA she became saved in general isolation, blindfolded, in a closet. This severe isolation and sensory deprivation endured for a while until the SLA commenced to tell Hearst that she could be killed.

Step by step, the group started to allow Hearst to enroll in with political discussions and she or he changed into at the end given the choice of joining the group. Simplest after confirming this became her choice became, she allowed disposing of her blindfold and lying eyes upon her captors. After her "Allegiance" changed into declared, Hearst started to go through intense narcotic and sexual torture inside the shape of rape and drug use.

The eventual outcome of this intense physical and political brainwashing turned into the previously respected and decent Hearst collaborating in various crimes on behalf of the SLA, together with documented bank robberies wherein she wielded a system gun and made violent threats toward the public.

One of the most exciting elements of the Hearst case is the empirical proof of brainwashing's impact that became available following her eventual arrest. Psychiatrists had been capable of conclusively show that following the brainwashing process, Hearst's IQ had dropped, and this amounted to a state wherein she turned into a "Zombie." This impact was so severe that Hearst had her sentence commuted and, in the end she received a complete Presidential pardon.

The brainwashing techniques of these extremist cults provide an unheard-of glimpse into the use and effect of dark psychology.

The KKK case looks at illustrates how brainwashing recruiters are capable of skillfully find a point of weak point in an individual's lifestyle and mercilessly exploit this to bend the victim to the organization's will. Their methods show how the precise ideological or political motivation at the back of brainwashing is hardly ever critical—a professional recruiter will be able to bend a susceptible sufferer to almost any perspective, given enough time and staying power.

Jonestown shows how isolation can cause utter insanity. Just as modern brainwashers, such as ISIS grow to be isolating people to the factor, they take their very own lifestyles for a political cause, Jonestown set up the blueprint for this very practice. The eventual quit sport of Jim Jones shows how for controlling cult leaders, the closing expression of their electricity and have an impact on is regularly the mass death of others.

The case of Patty Hearst and the SLA indicates how brainwashing can take a greater forceful and speedy path than the conventional path of graduality. Its miles testament to the power of Stockholm syndrome that Hearst seemed to "Willingly" act according to the pastimes of her captors, even if she was not physically constrained. This is a clear sign that the mental shackles imposed with the aid of a brainwasher are far extra powerful than any physical chains ought to ever be.

CHAPTER 12
CONCLUSION

We've Learned

You presently have a map of the maximum risky minds to ever have existed.

The standards that undermine the arena of dark psychology. You understand how these principles are applied and changed to extraordinary conditions. You can apprehend the tendencies of the people most probably to be, in search to exert their mental powers over you.

Clean case studies have provided perception into the outer limits of Dark psychology and the manner it has been implemented during human history.

Protective Sword?

Every reader of this eBook can have had a slightly different enjoyment.

Did you get the feel of getting to know effective shielding techniques and thoughts you can use to shield yourself and your family from the evil of the arena?

Possibly turned into your joy of a touch...Darker? A bit exciting? Perhaps in the experience you presently have, a valuable secret weapon you could use to get ahead inside the world.

Anything your experience has been, you understand now the truth of existence. There is no going lower back.

This eBook can be considered a rulebook for the true game of existence.

No matter which way you need to play is entirely as much as you.